Fantasy & Fashion
a coloring book

Timothy R. Cook

Fantasy & Fashion: a coloring book

Copyright © 2018 Timothy R. Cook

http://www.etsy.com/shop/TimCookArt

ISBN: 1987736885
ISBN-13: 978-1987736885

Printed by CreateSpace, an Amazon.com company.

All rights reserved. No part of this book may be used or reproduced in any manner except for personal, noncommercial purposes without written permission from the author.

Cover and interior illustrations by Timothy R. Cook.

Acknowledgments & Inspiration

Alphonse Mucha's art is the primary source of inspiration for the technical style and fashion design of these drawings, and the graceful elegance and inherent strength of ballet with its fluid lines of form and motion are the most important stylistic influences. Elements of high fashion designers such as Zuuhair Murad, Paolo Sebastian, Ralph and Russo, and others have also contributed to the clothing designs herein.

Part I

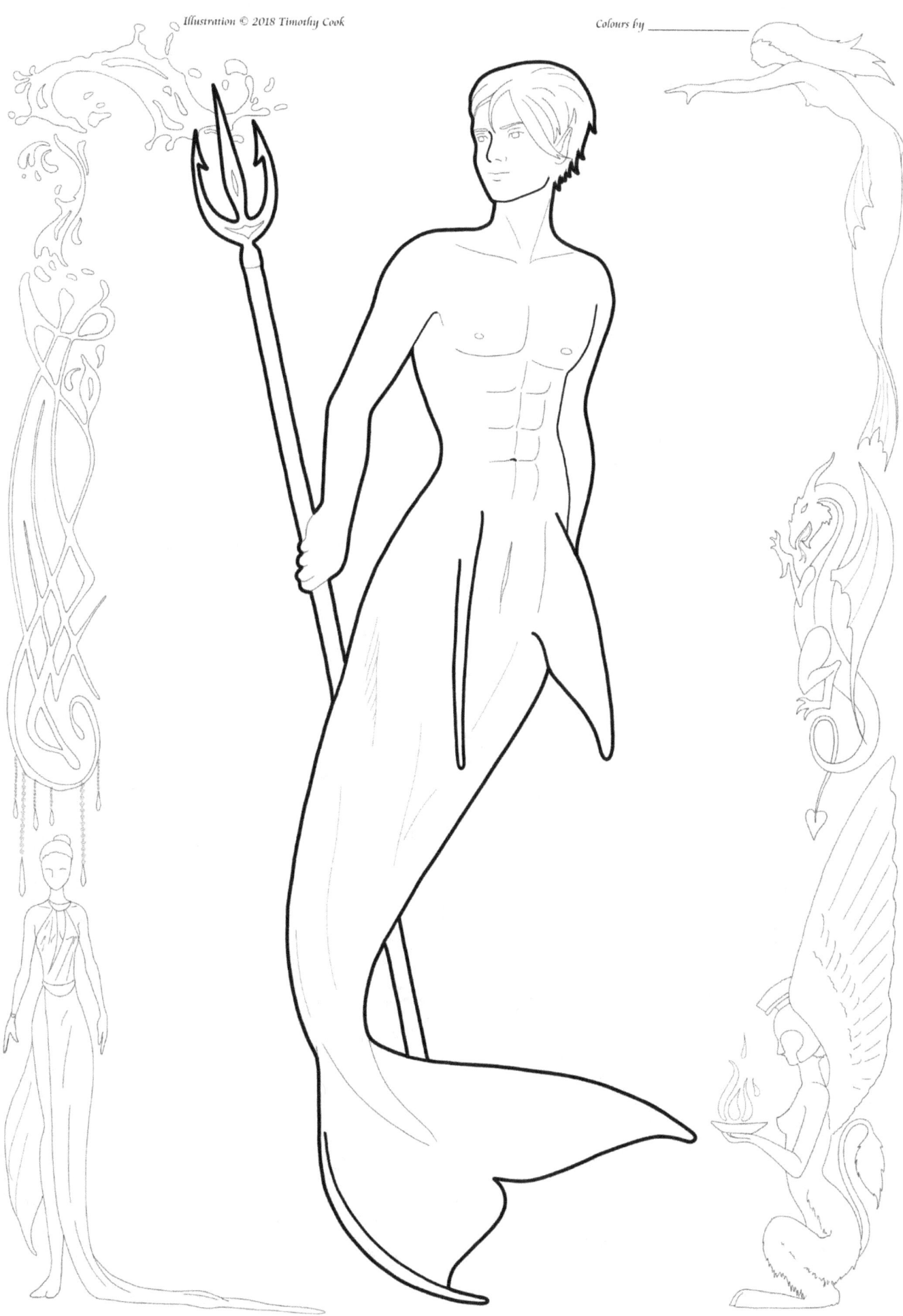

Illustration © 2018 Timothy Cook   Colours by _____

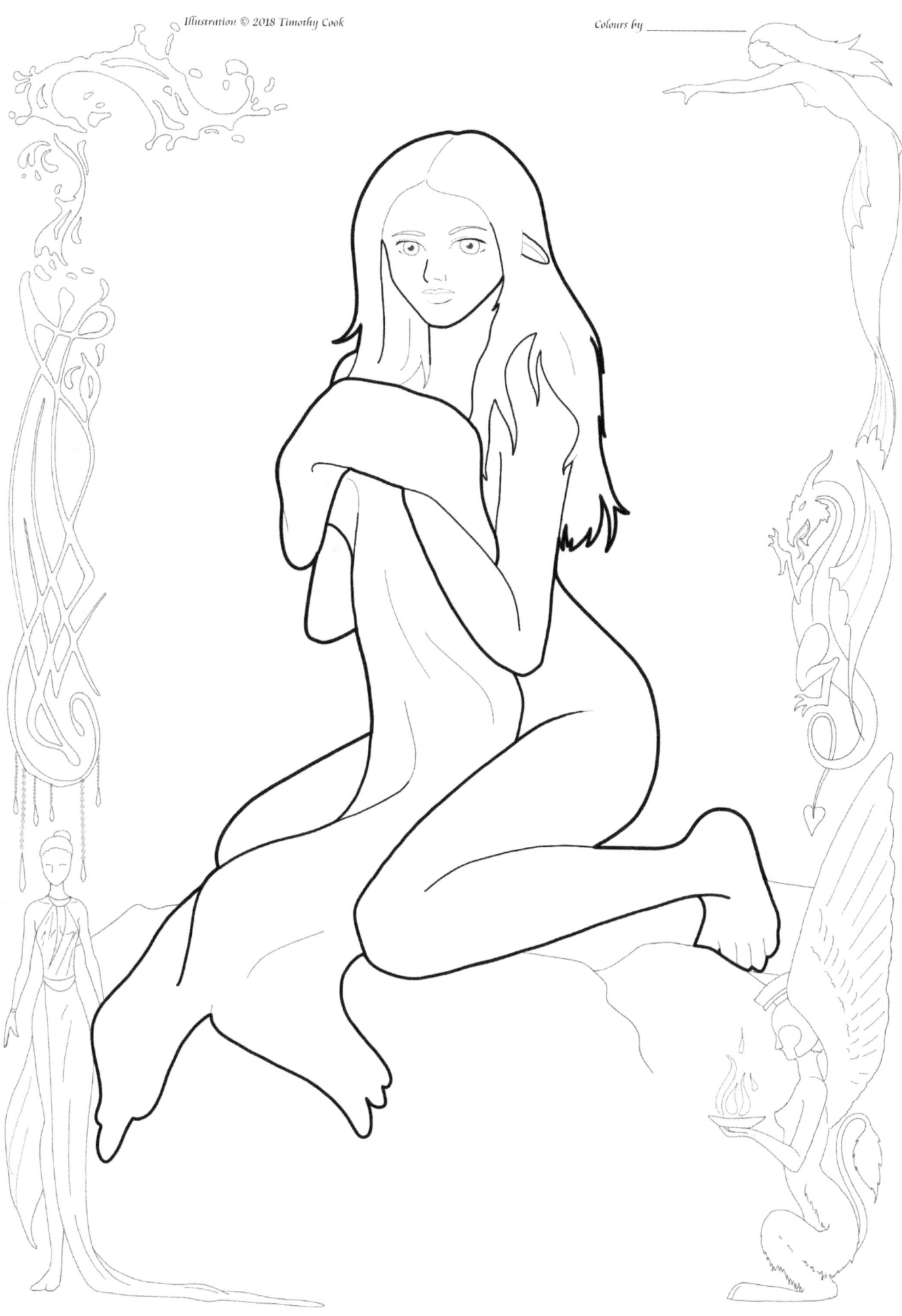

Illustration © 2018 Timothy Cook   Colours by _____

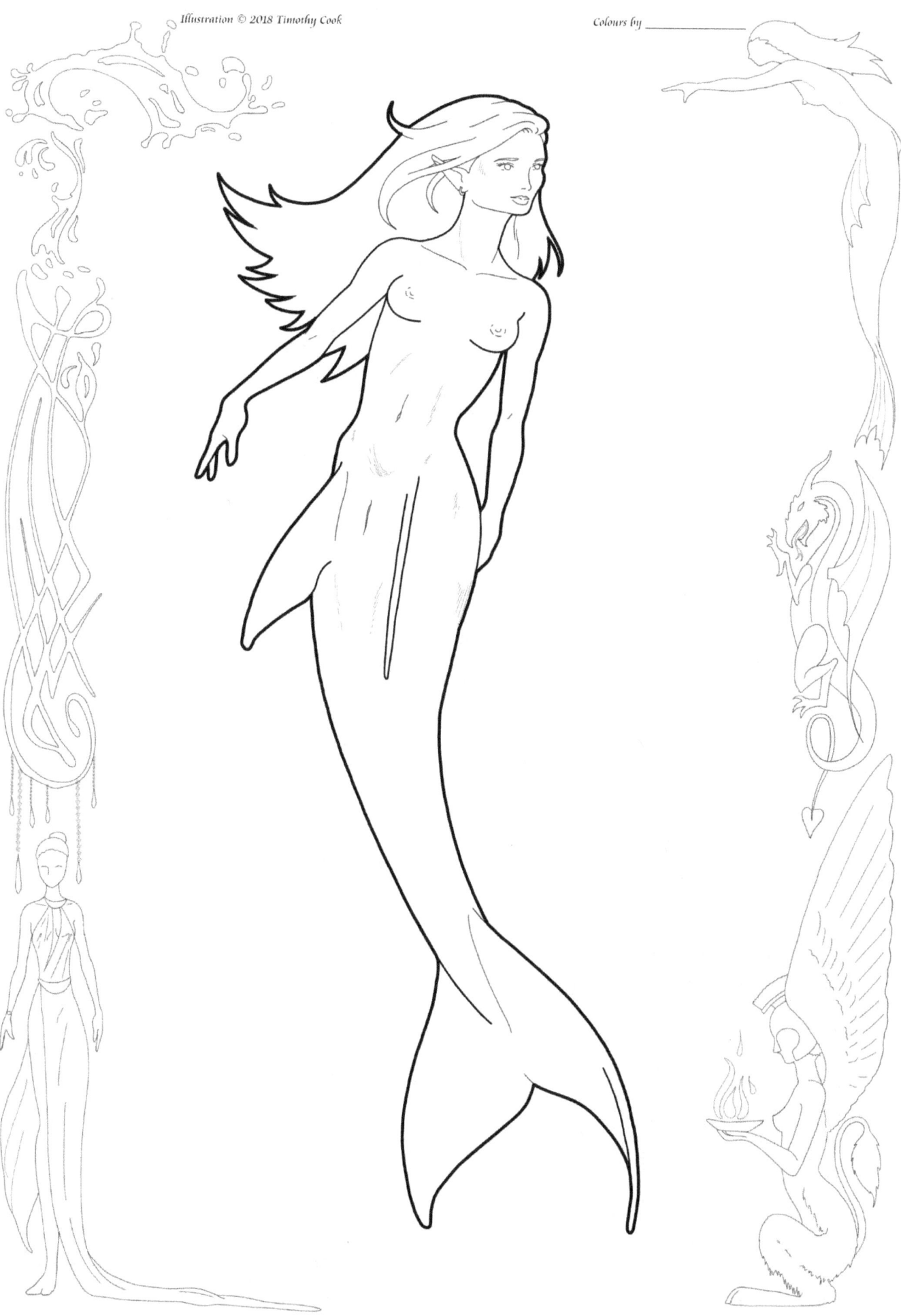

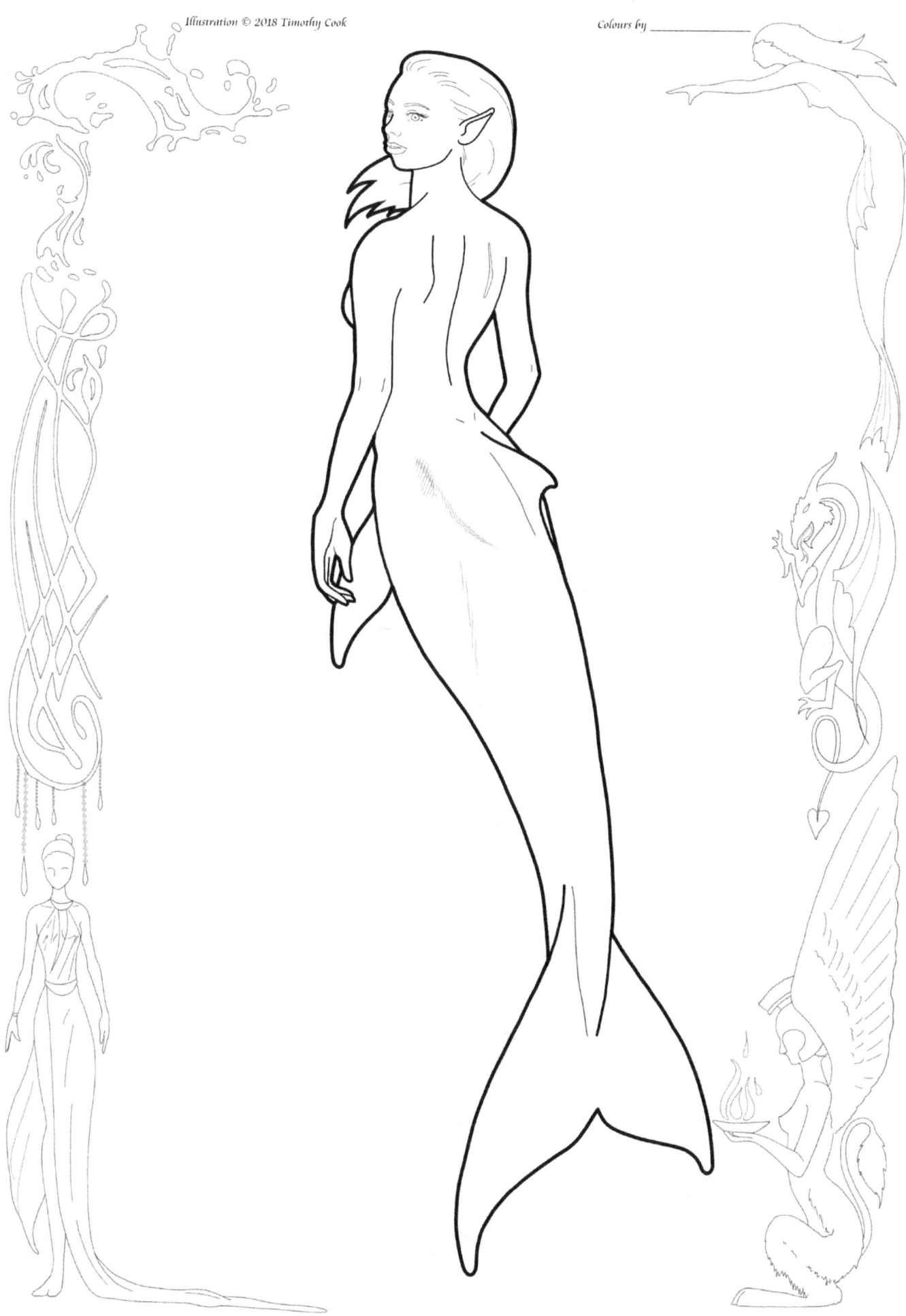

Illustration © 2018 Timothy Cook   Colours by _____

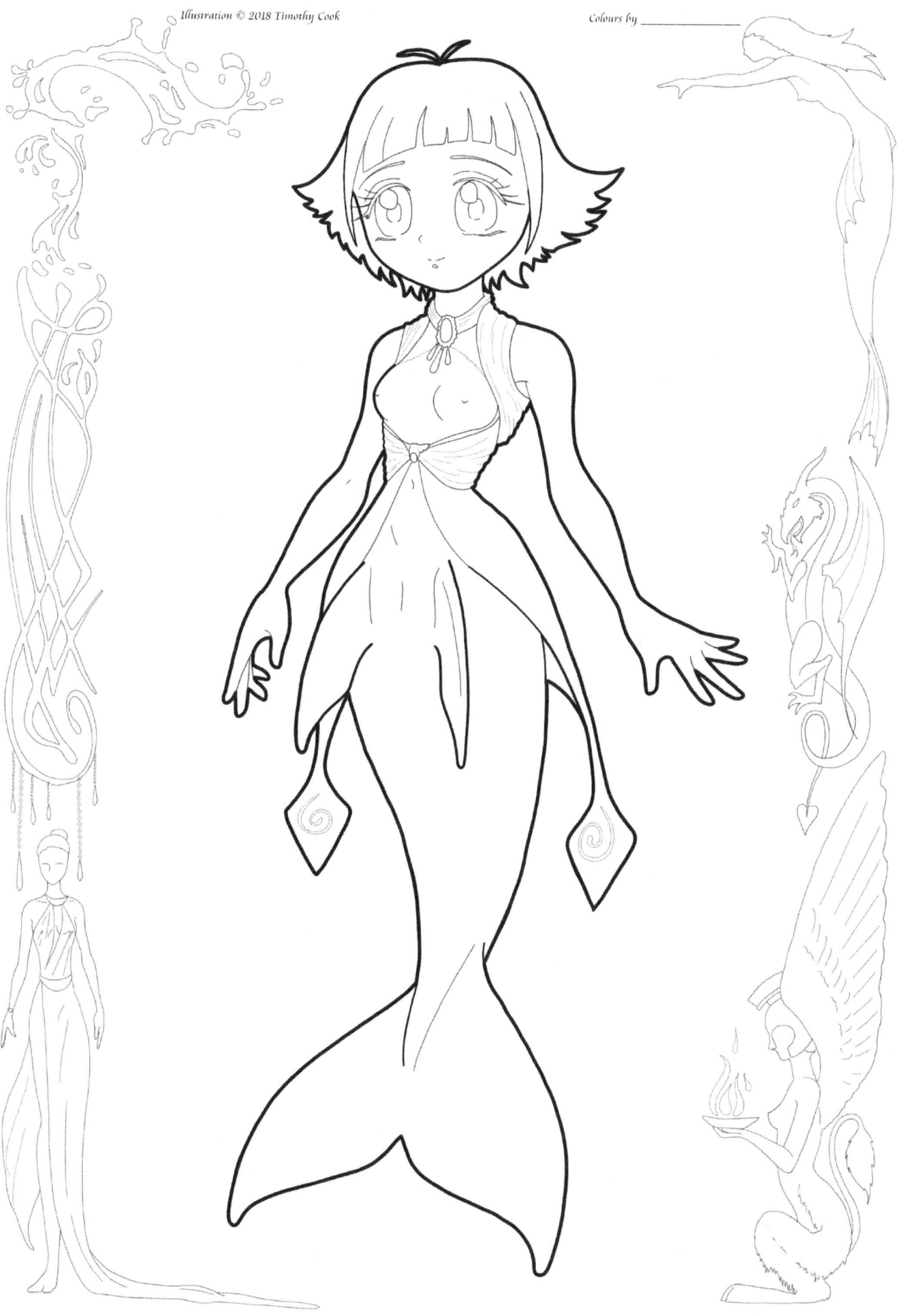

Illustration © 2018 Timothy Cook Colours by _____

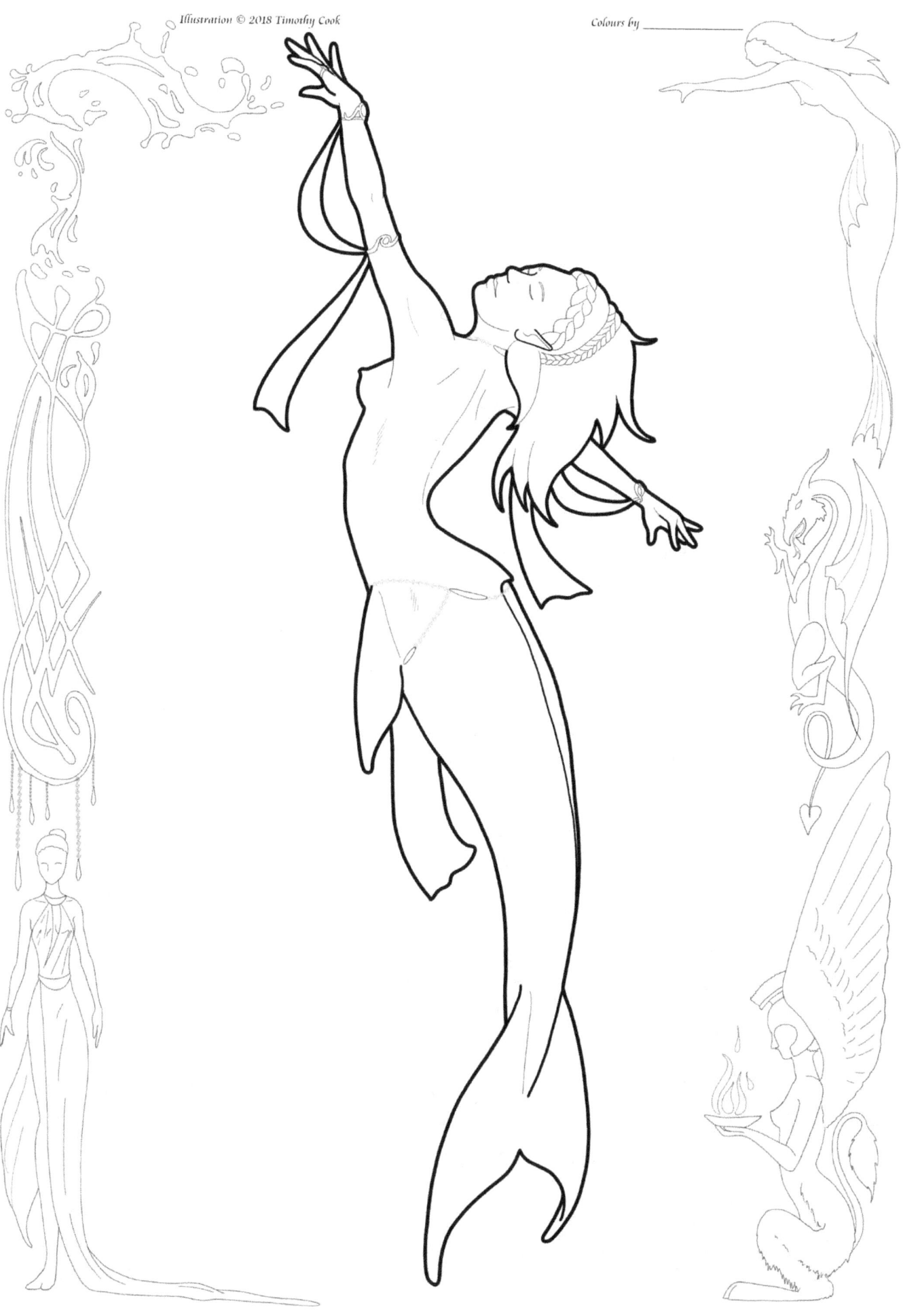

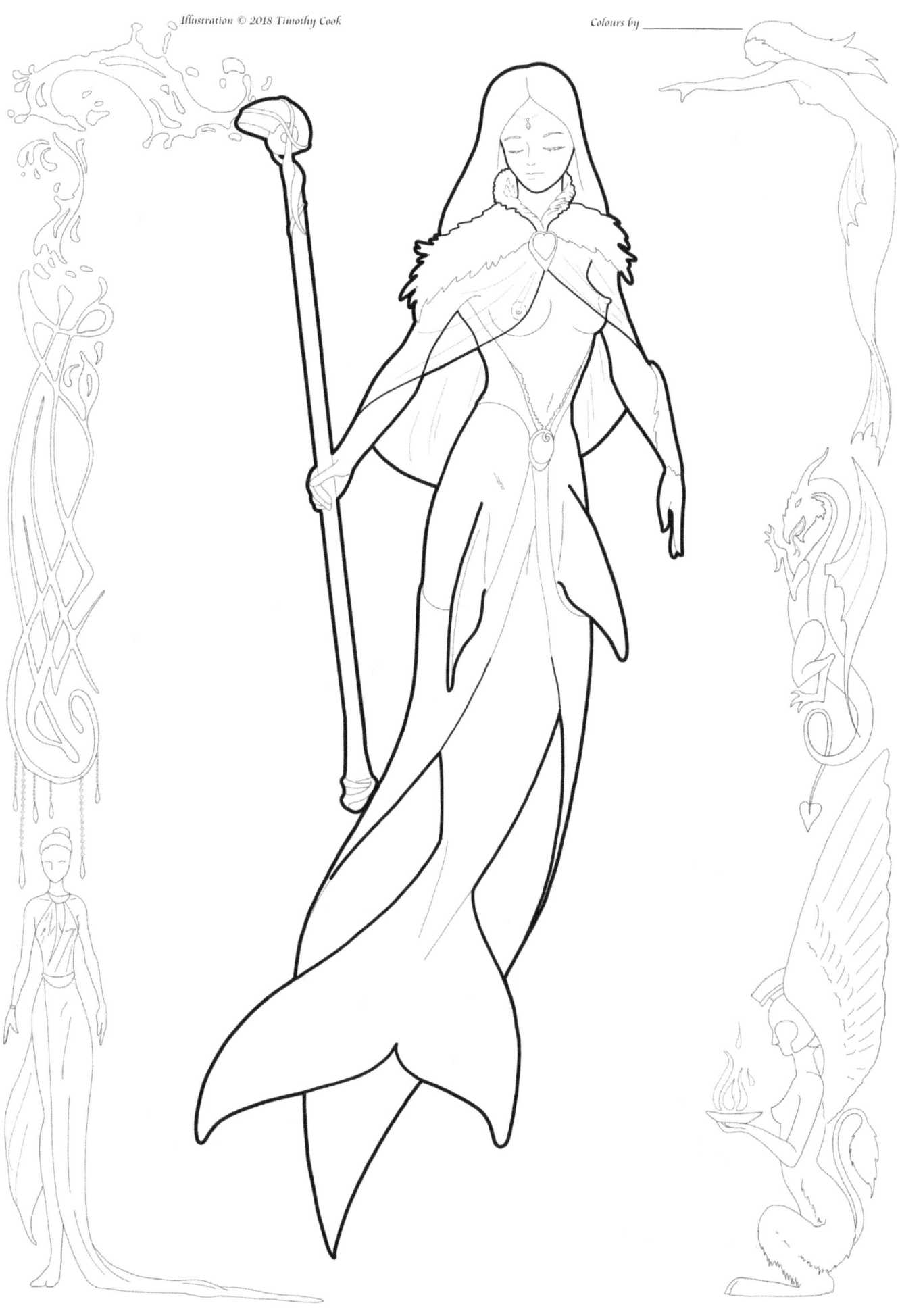

Illustration © 2018 Timothy Cook
Colours by _____

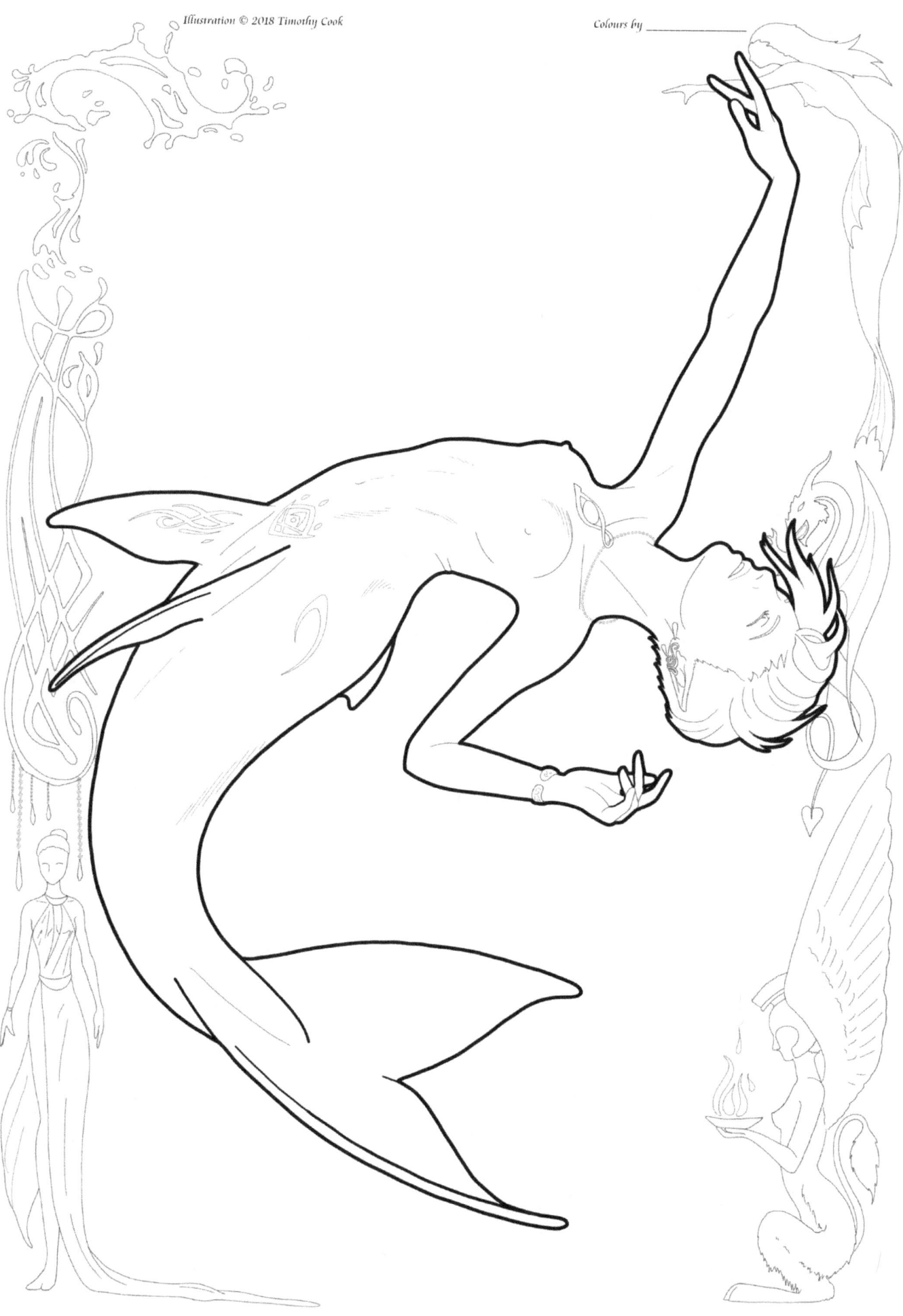

Illustration © 2018 Timothy Cook   Colours by _____

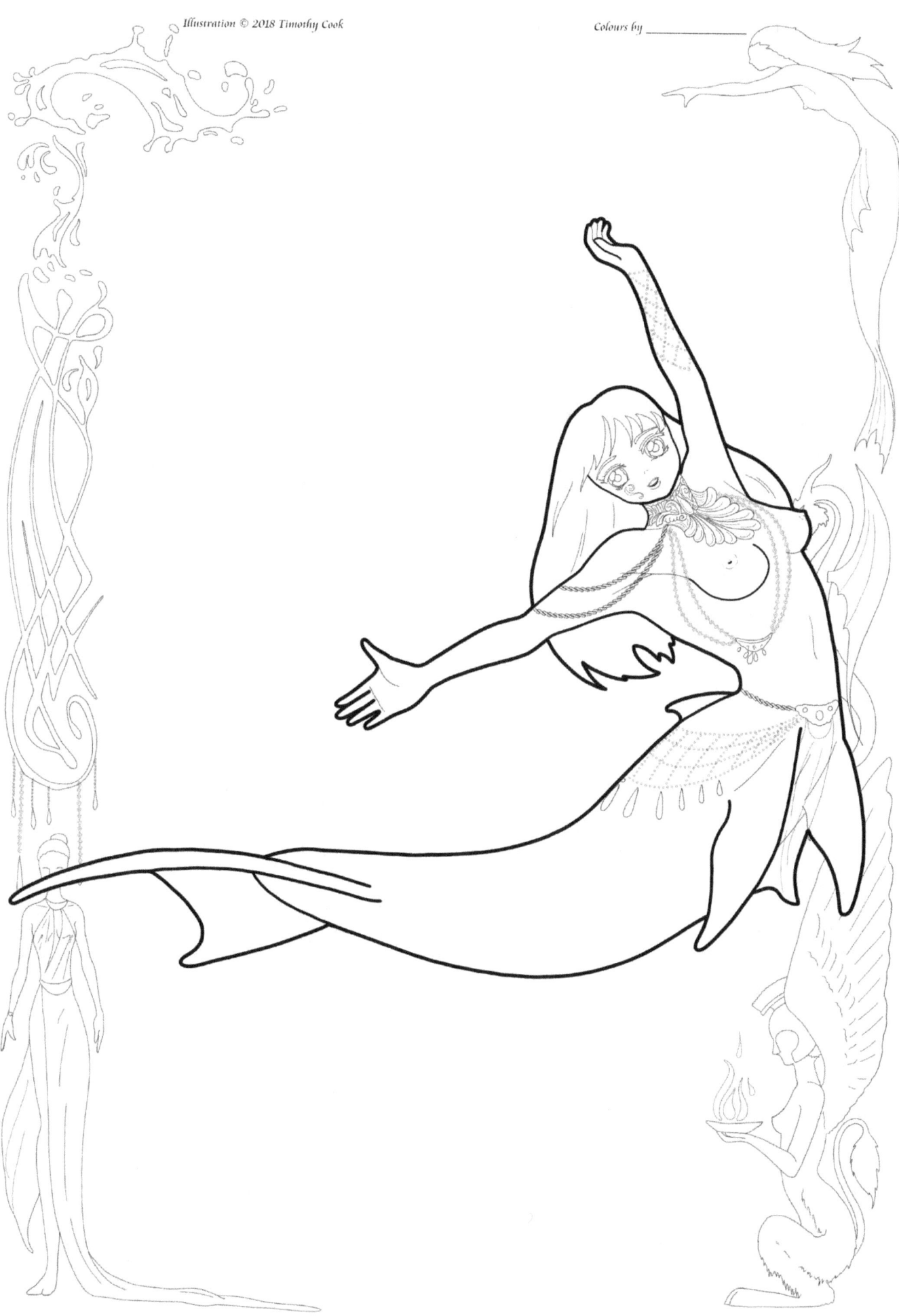

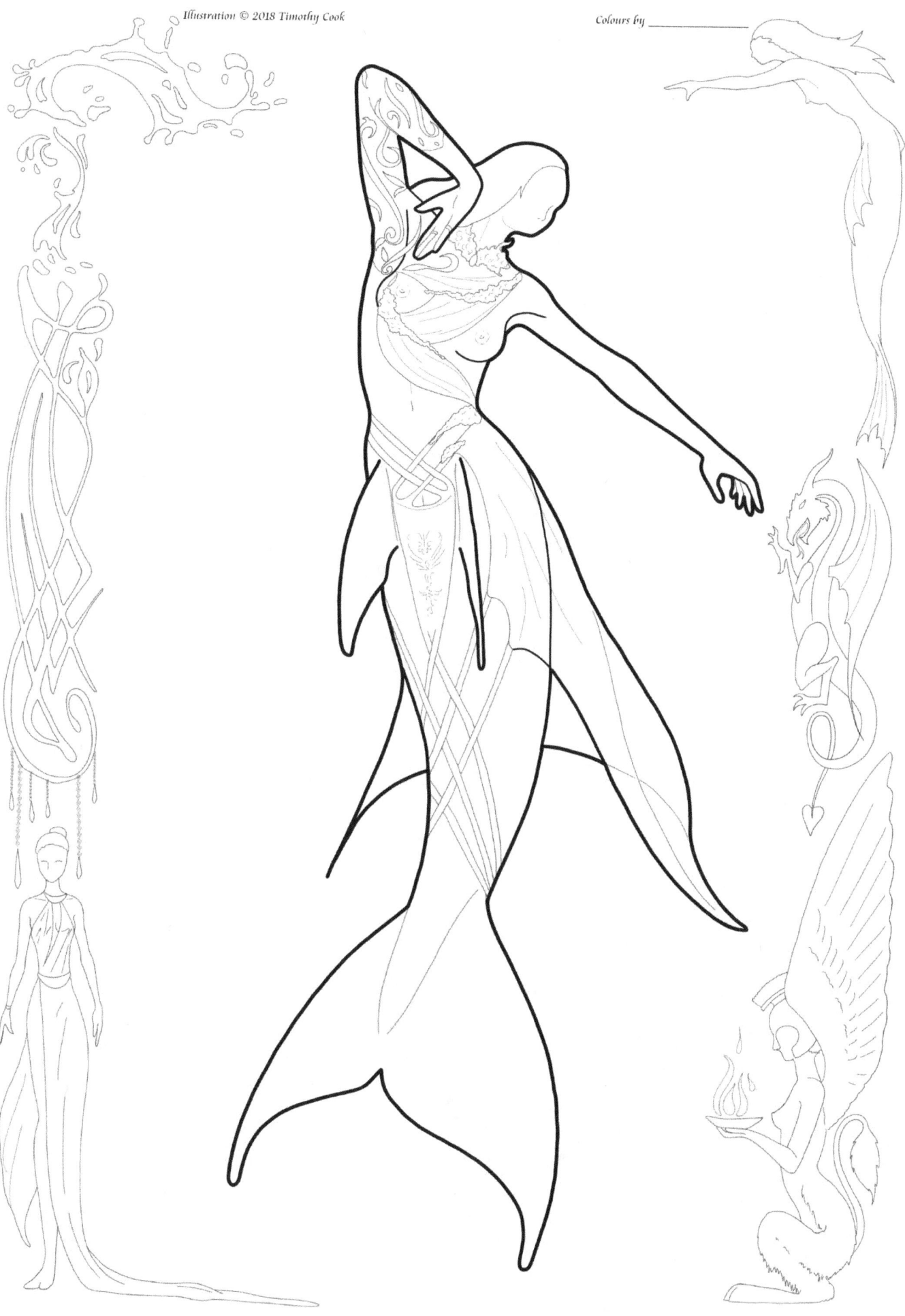

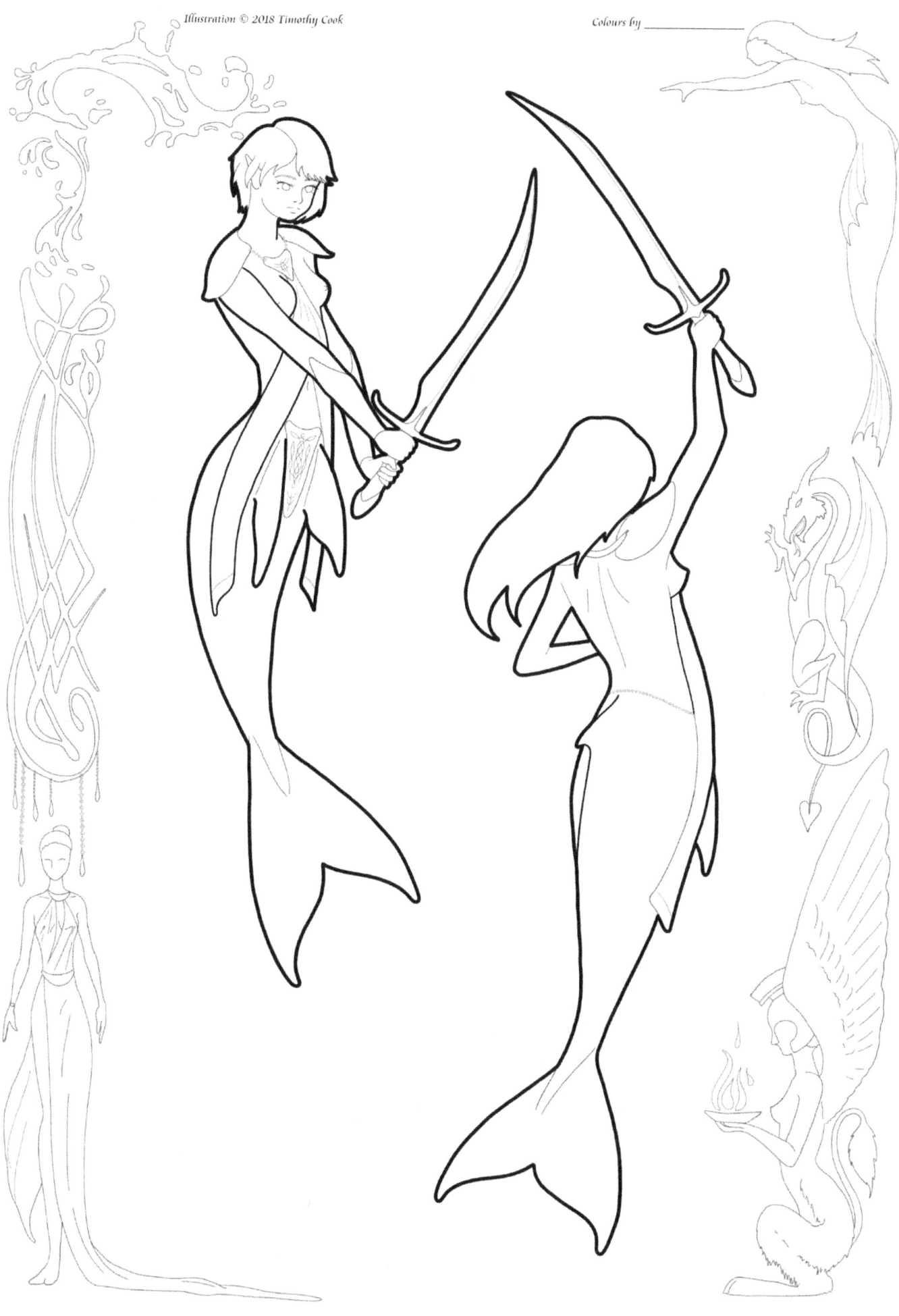

Part II

Illustration © 2018 Timothy Cook Colours by _____

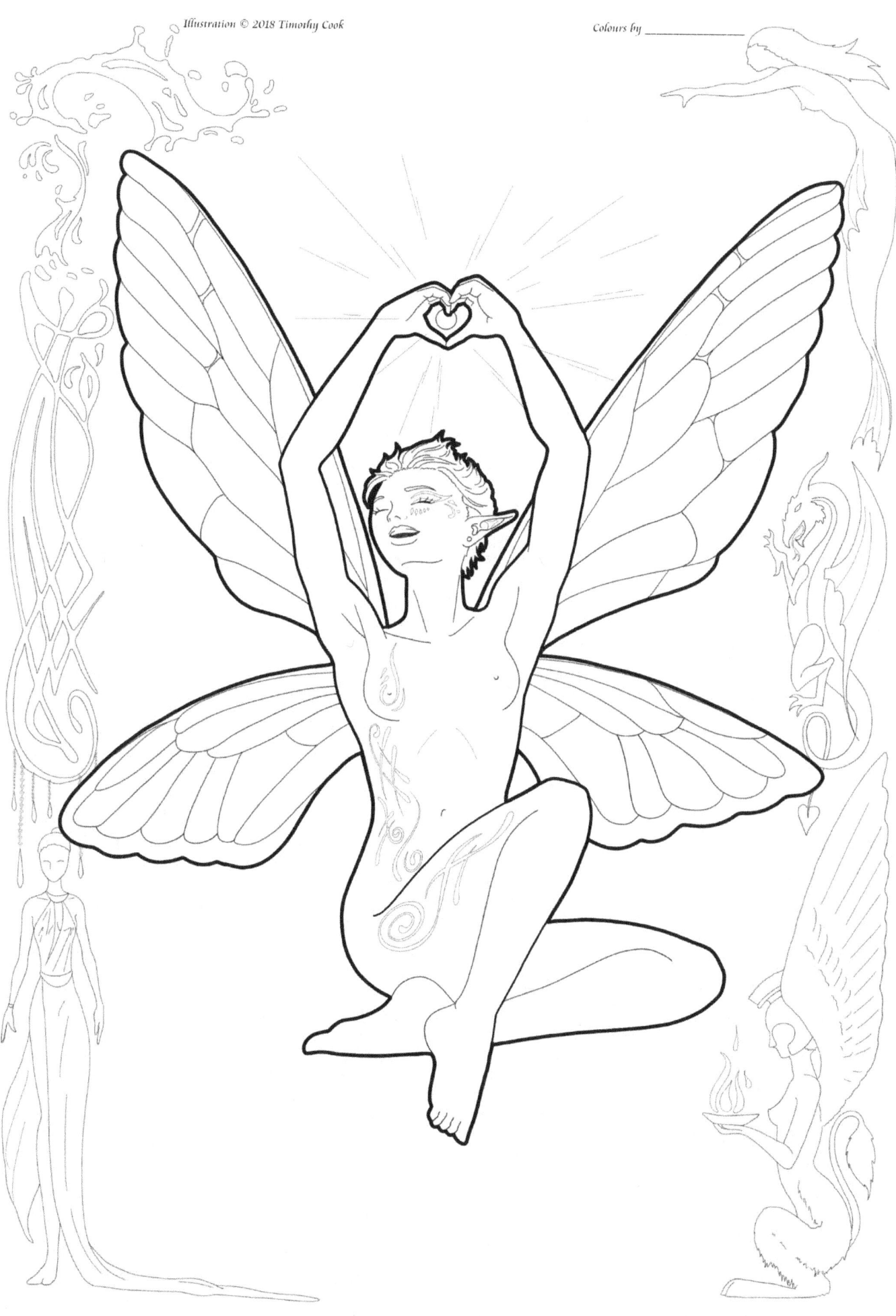

Illustration © 2018 Timothy Cook   Colours by _____

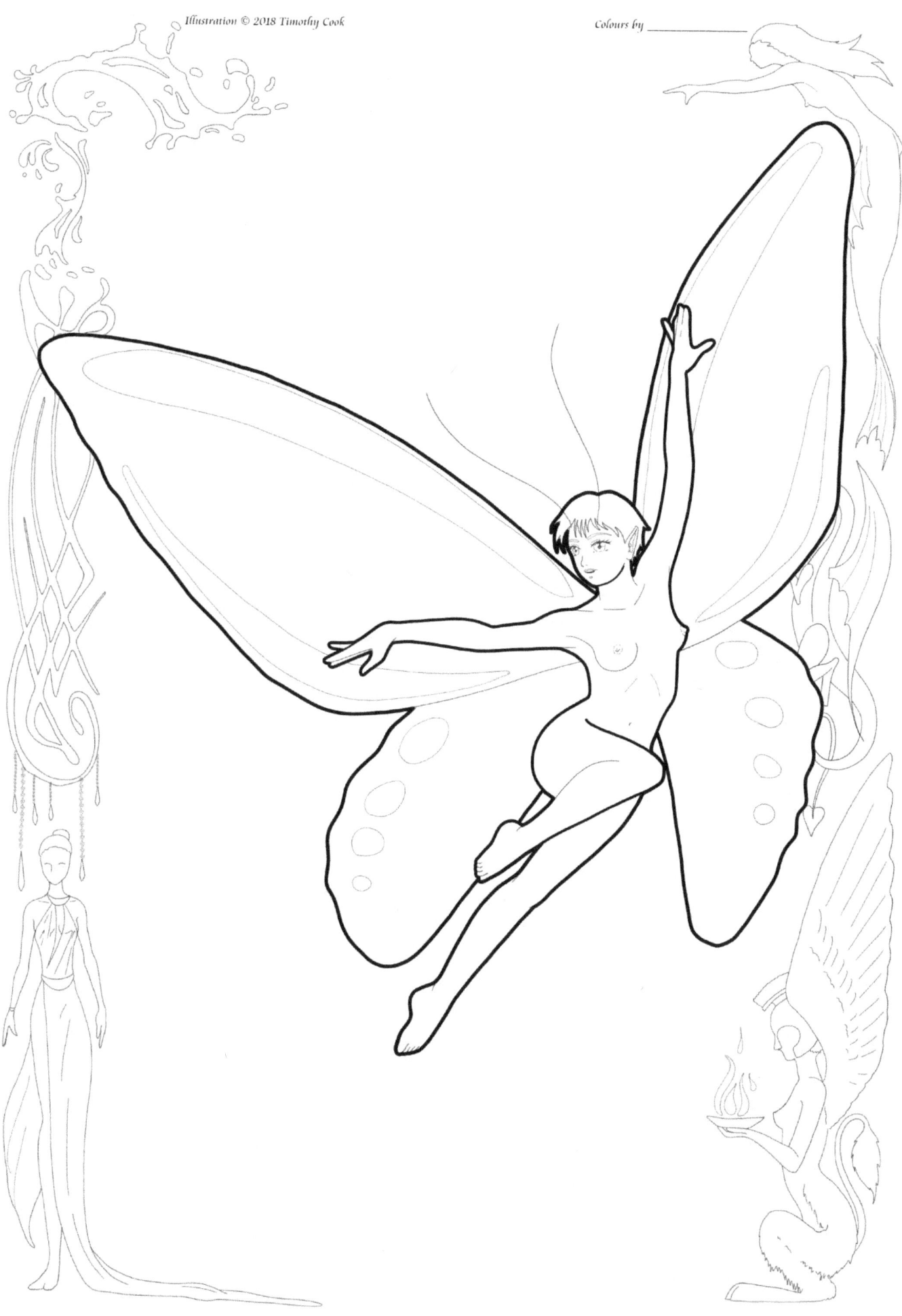

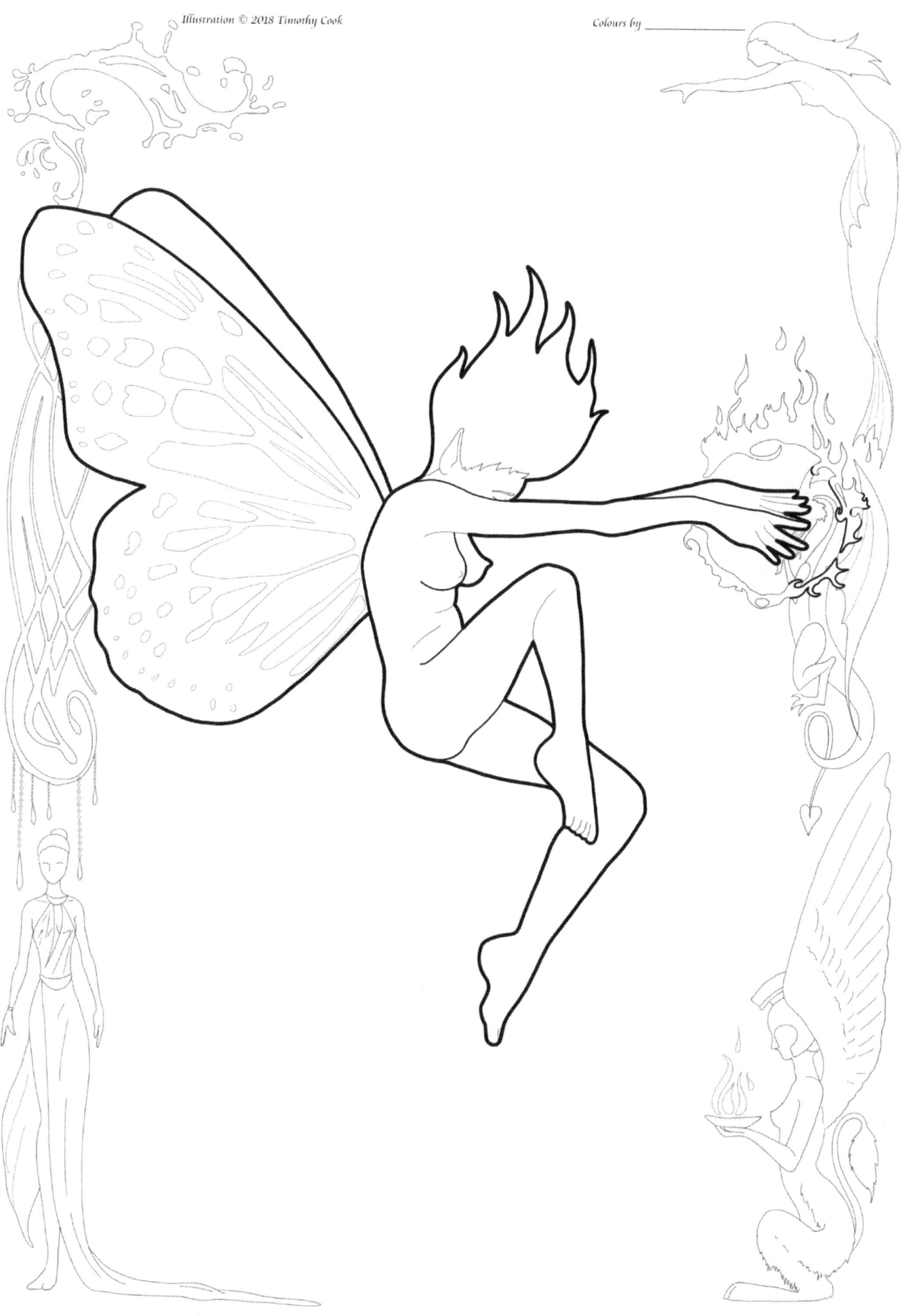

Illustration © 2018 Timothy Cook   Colours by _____

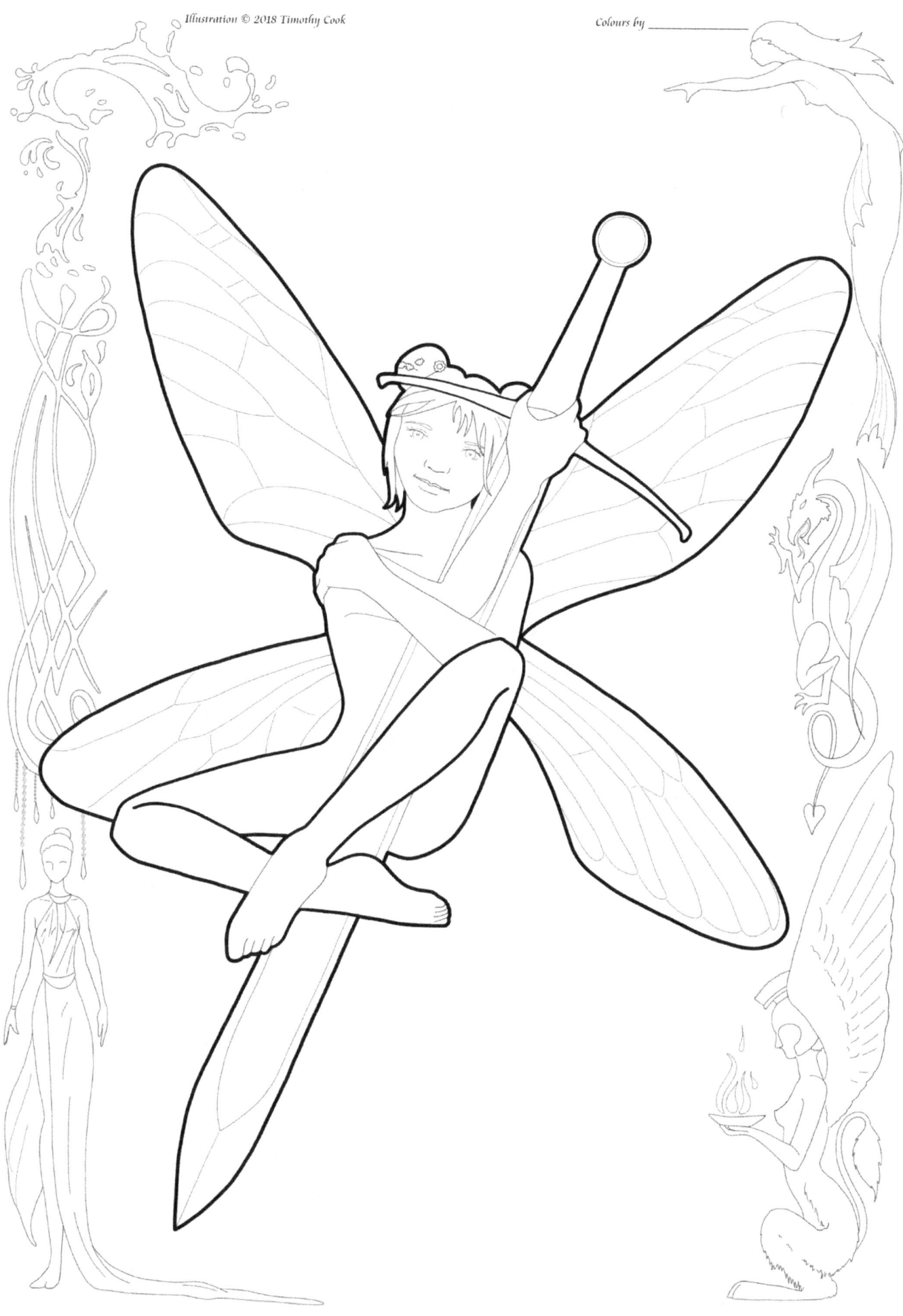

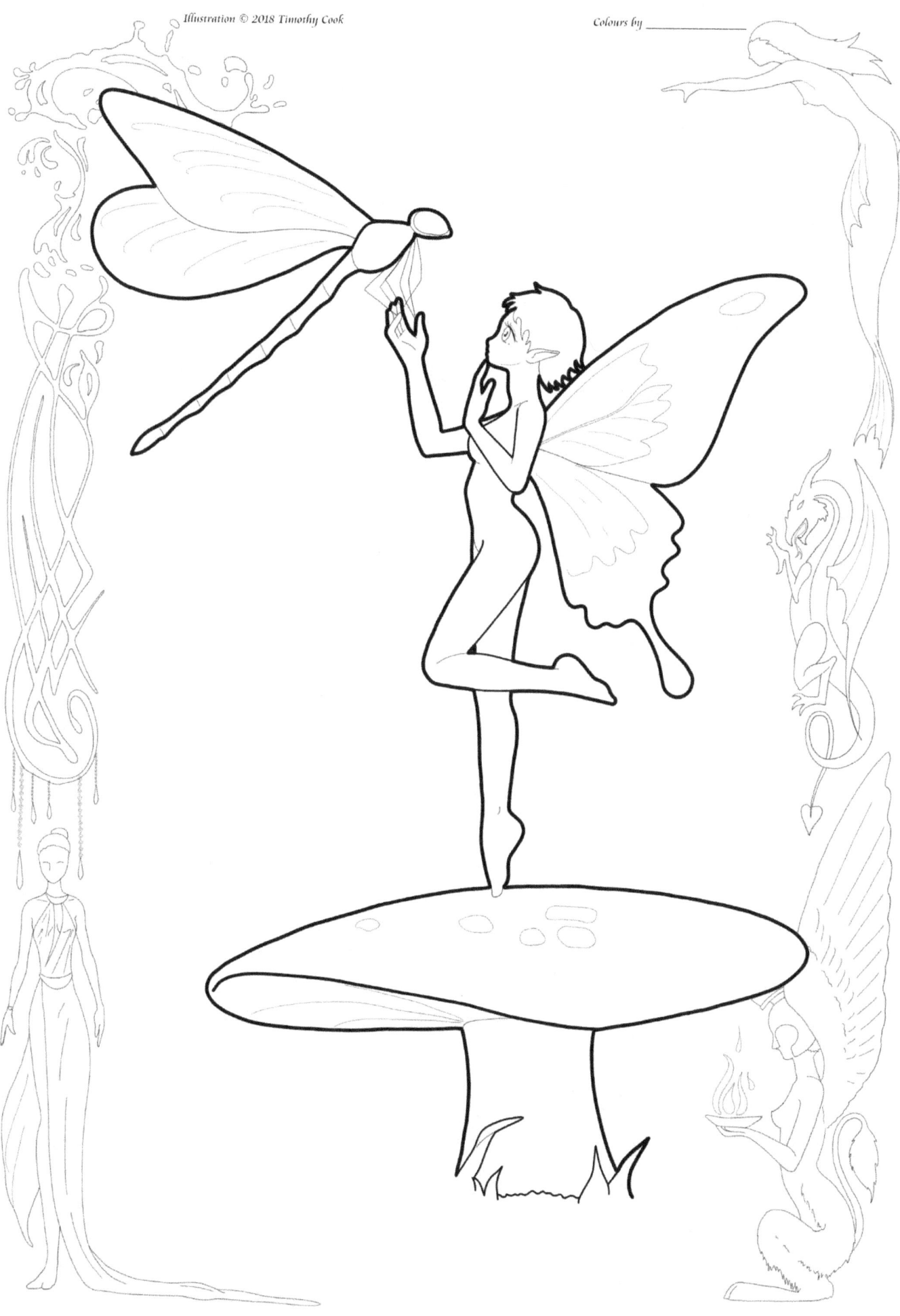

Illustration © 2018 Timothy Cook Colours by _____

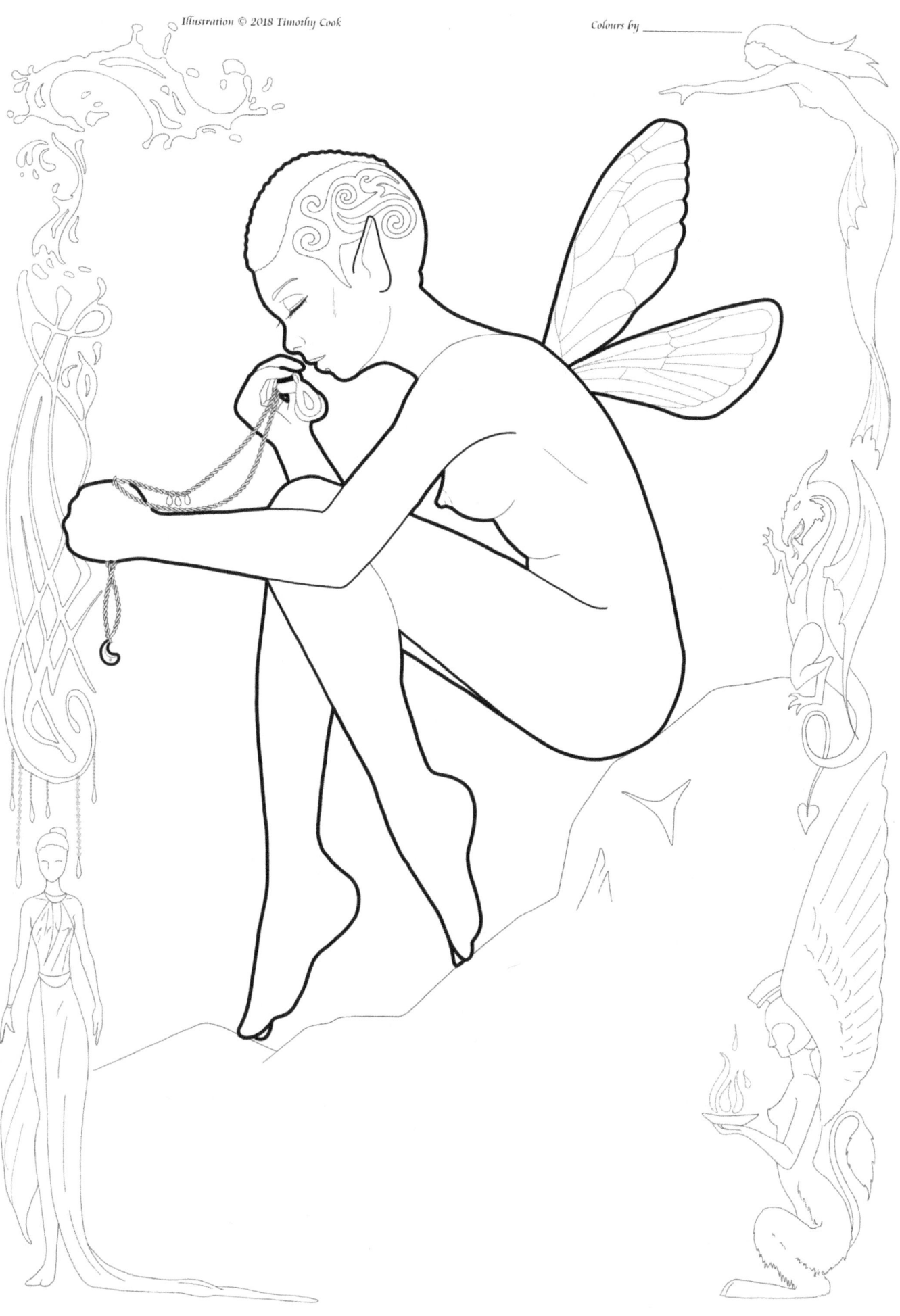

Illustration © 2018 Timothy Cook   Colours by _____

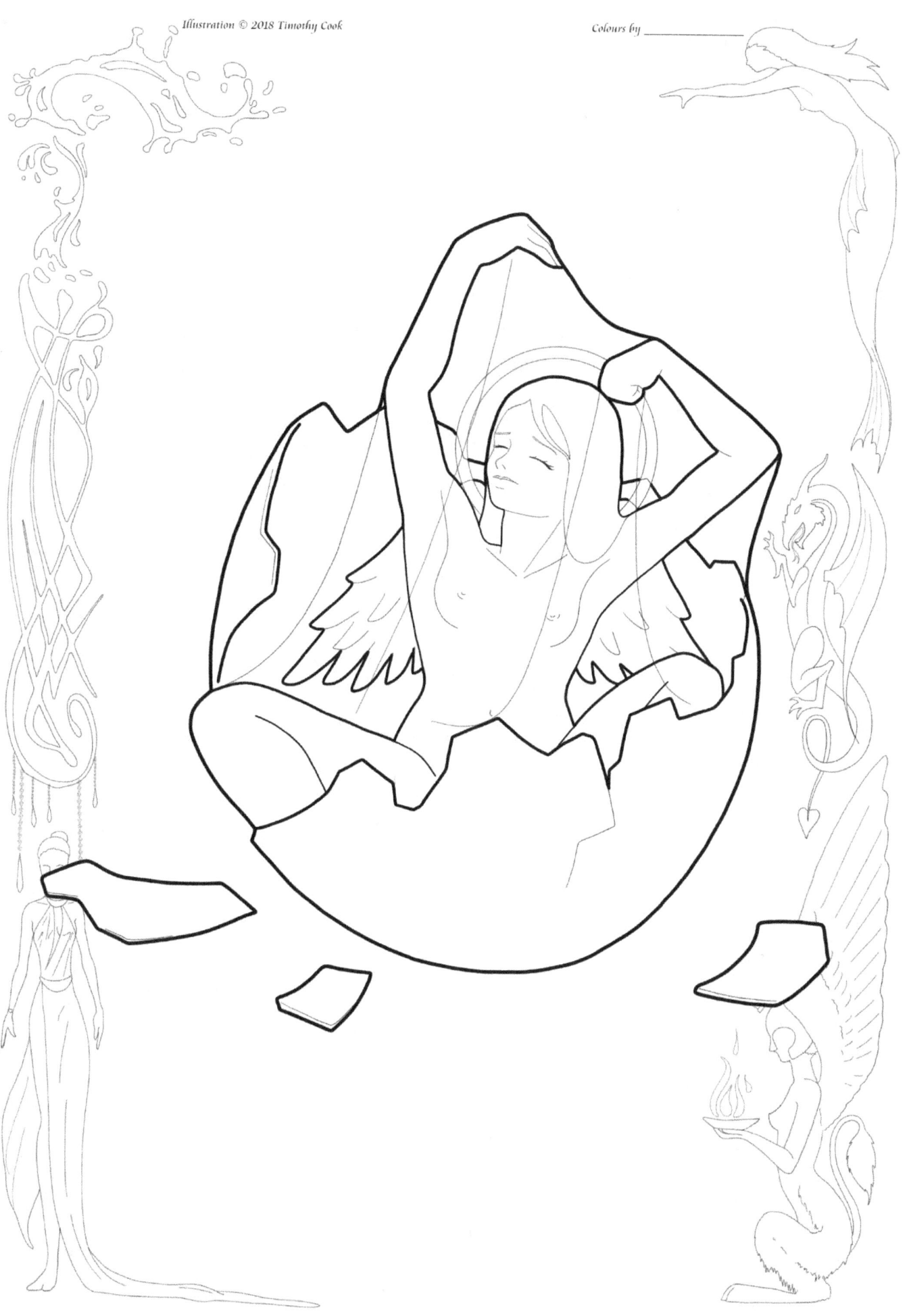

Illustration © 2018 Timothy Cook Colours by _____

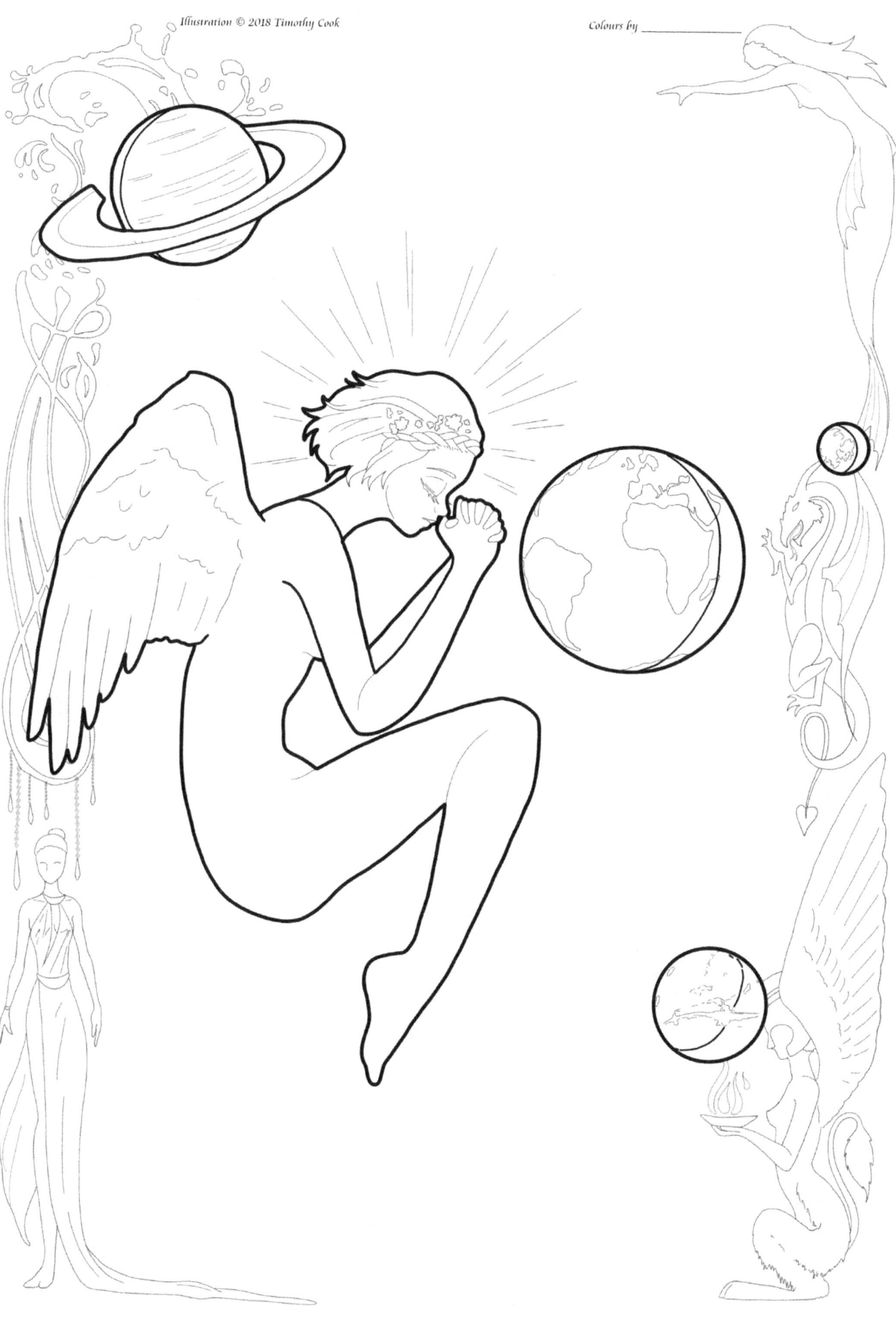

Illustration © 2018 Timothy Cook   Colours by _____

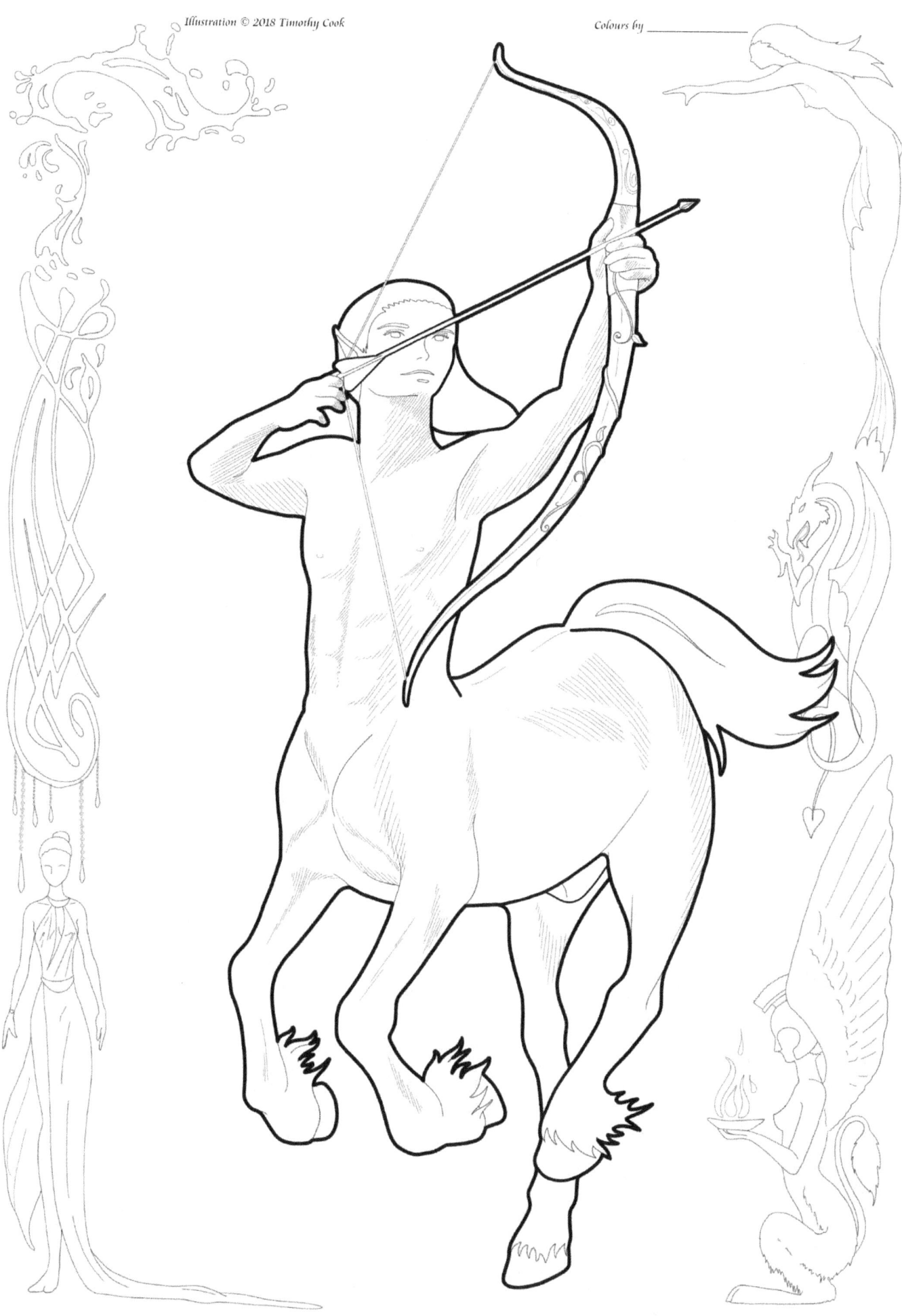

Illustration © 2018 Timothy Cook   Colours by _____

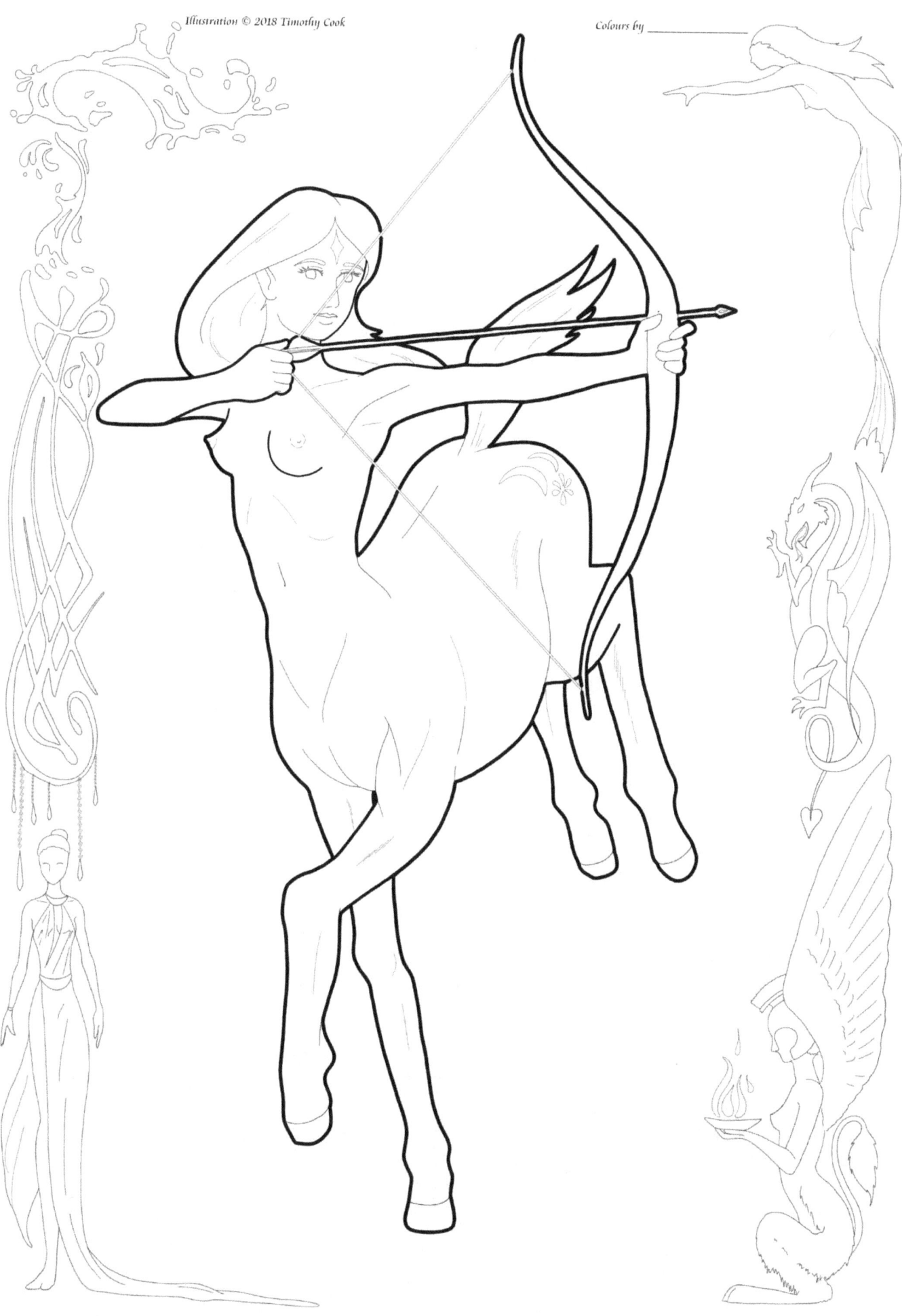

Illustration © 2018 Timothy Cook   Colours by _____

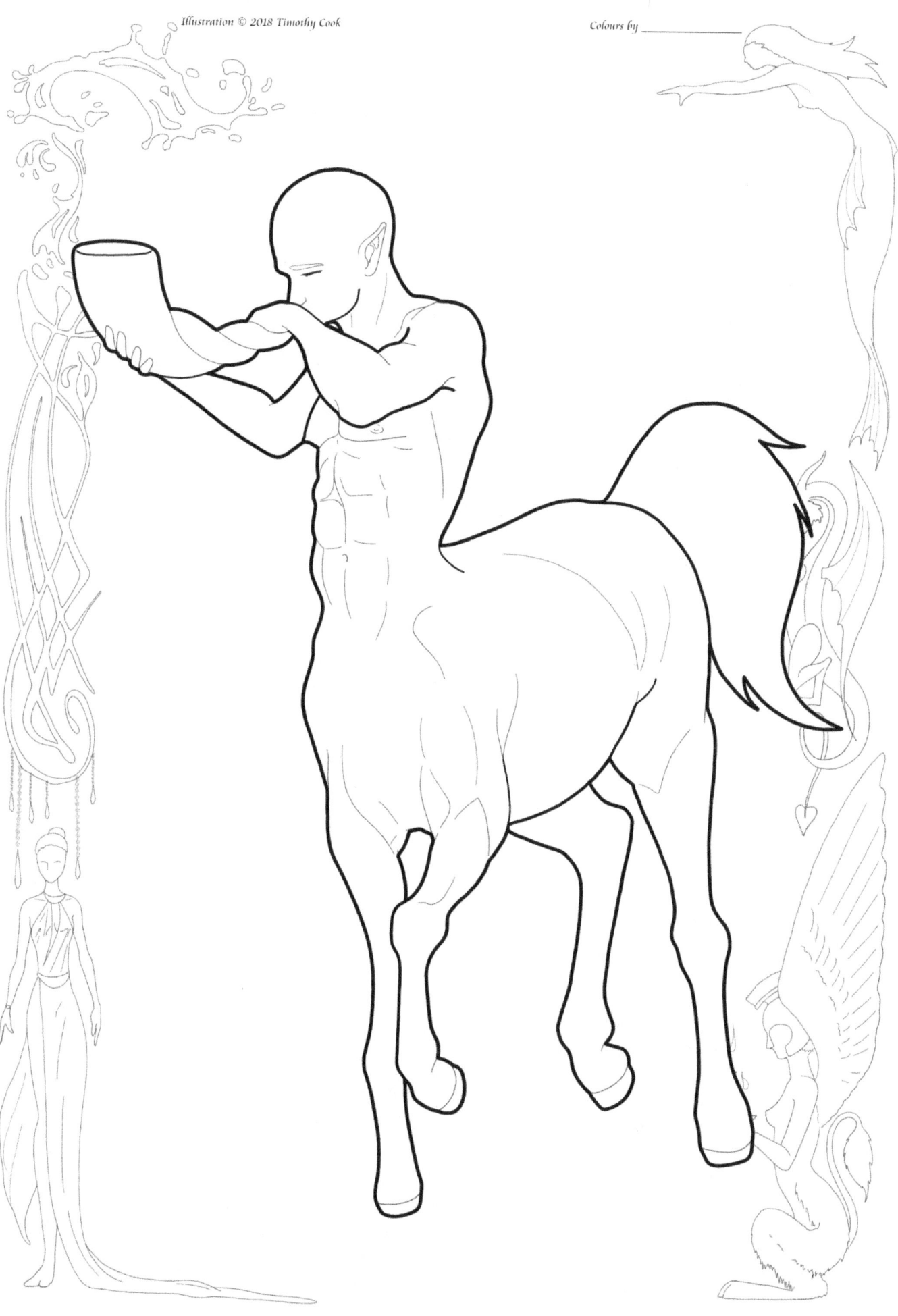

Illustration © 2018 Timothy Cook   Colours by _____

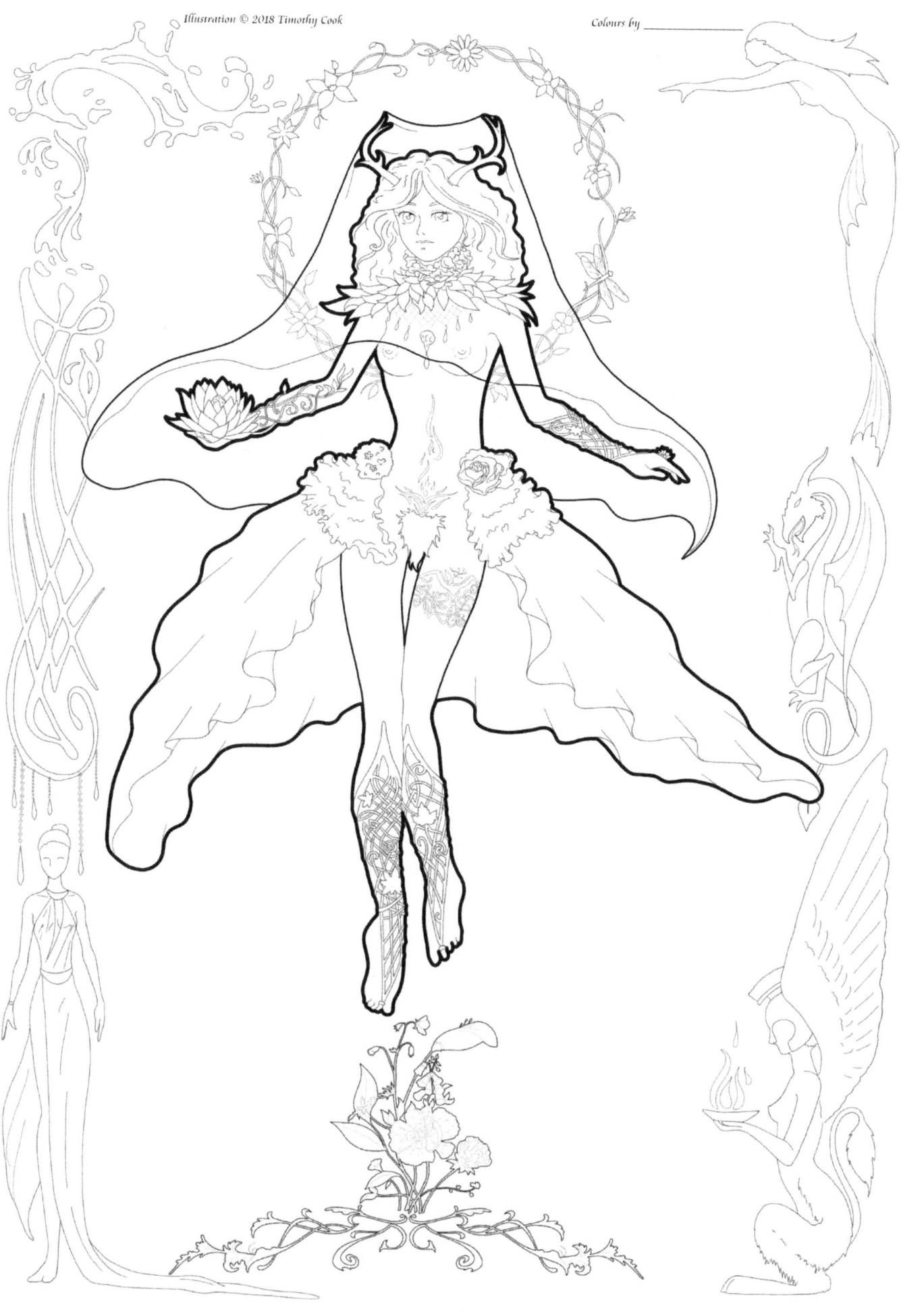

Illustration © 2018 Timothy Cook Colours by _____

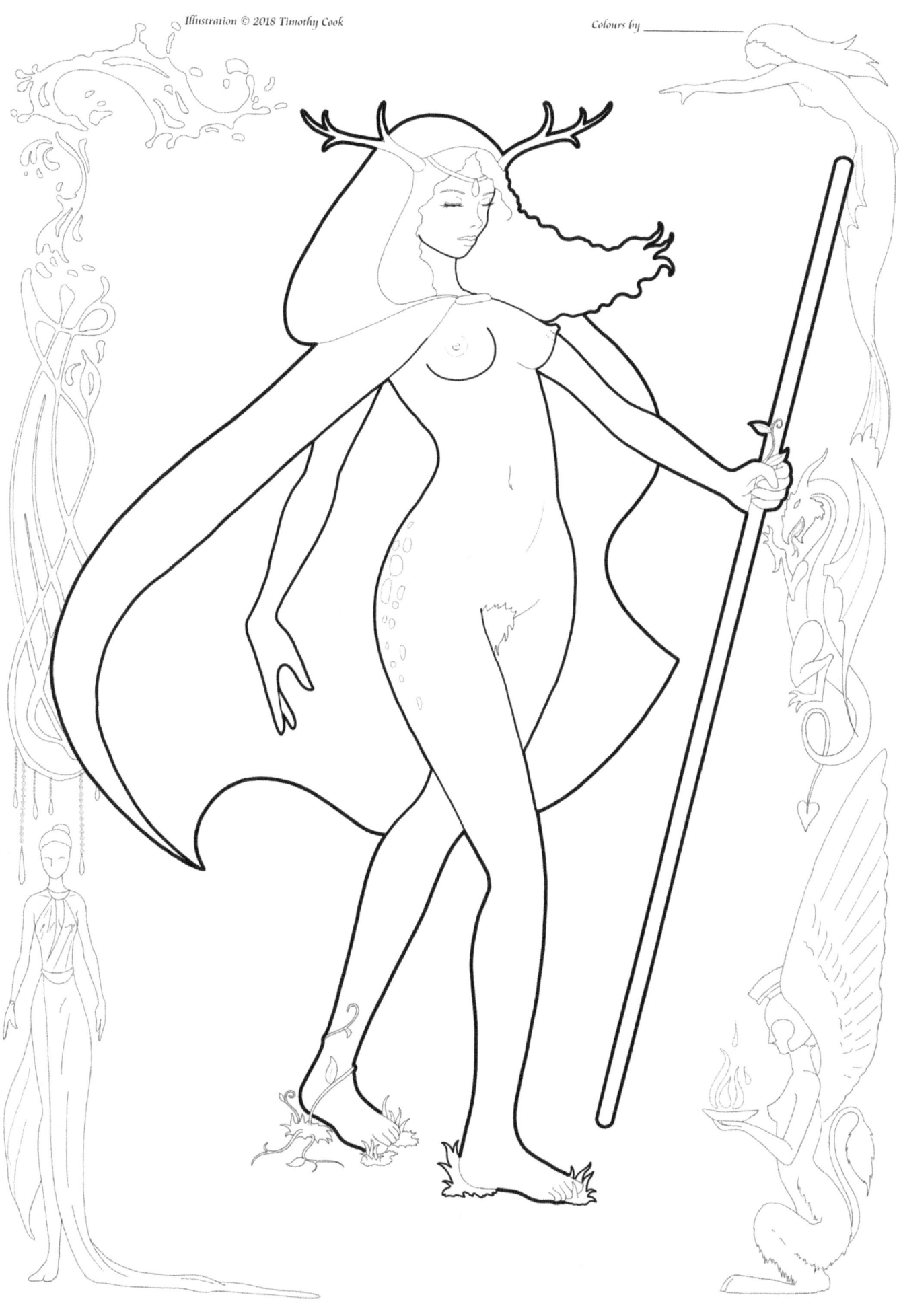

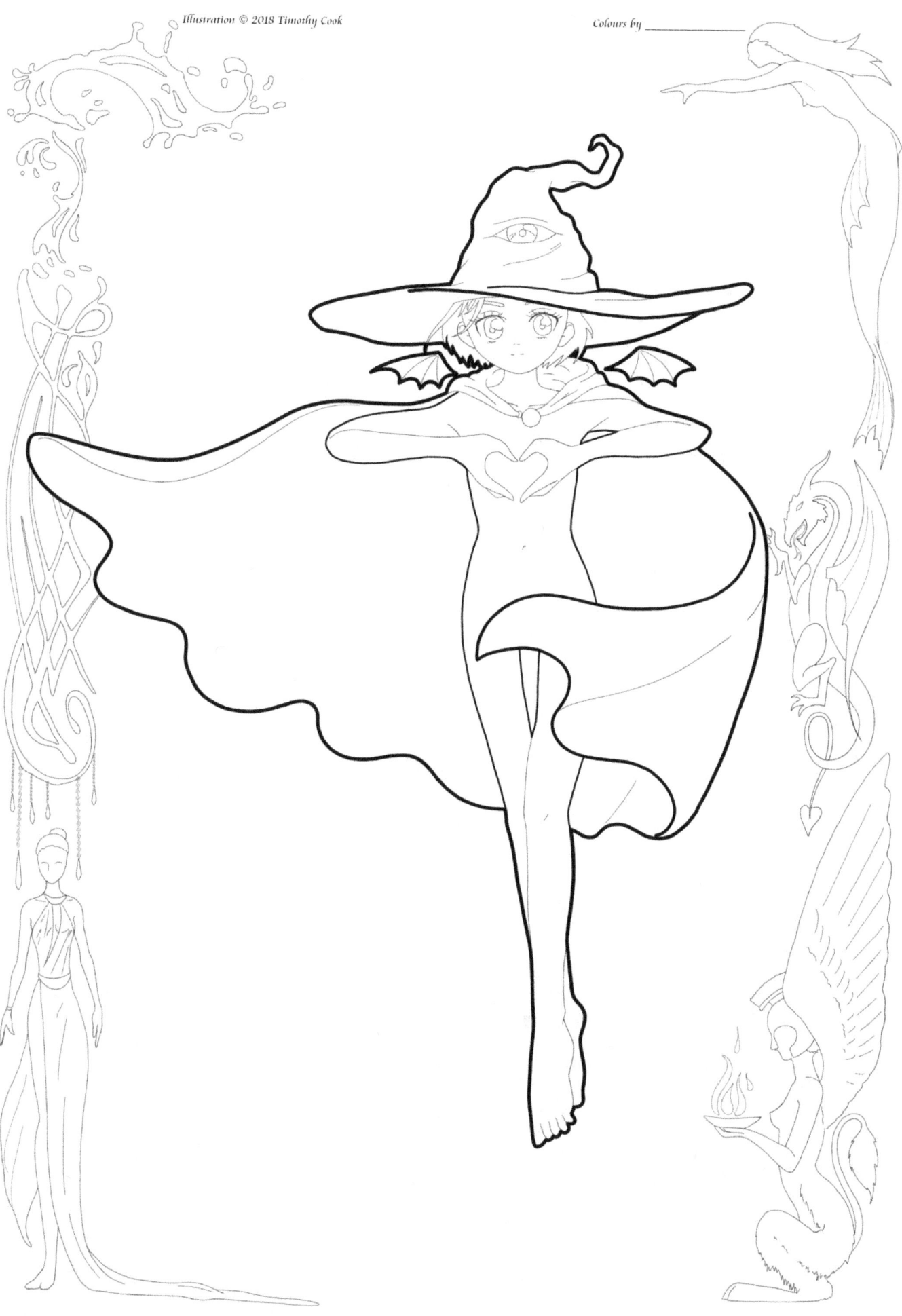

Part III

Illustration © 2018 Timothy Cook   Colours by _____

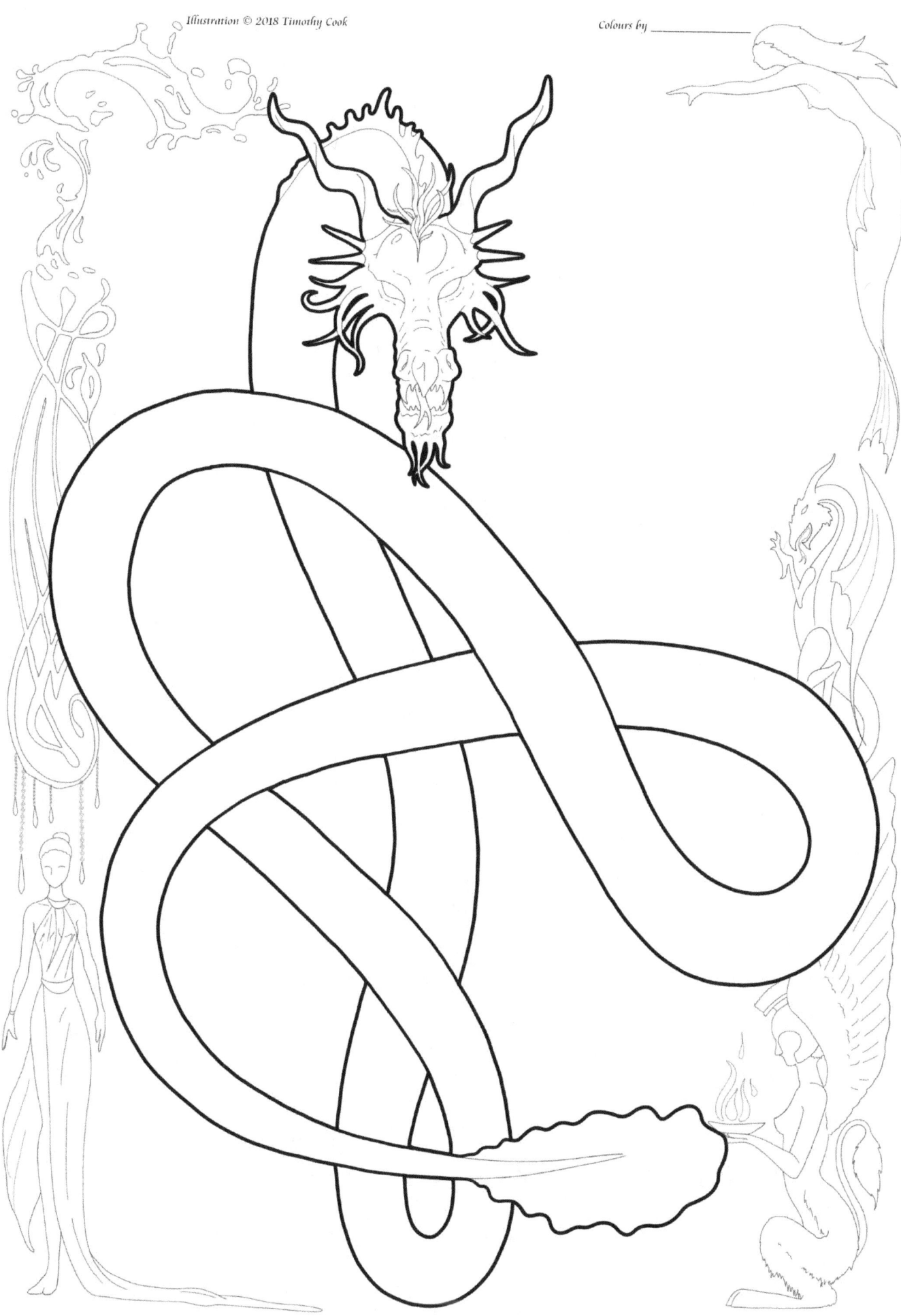

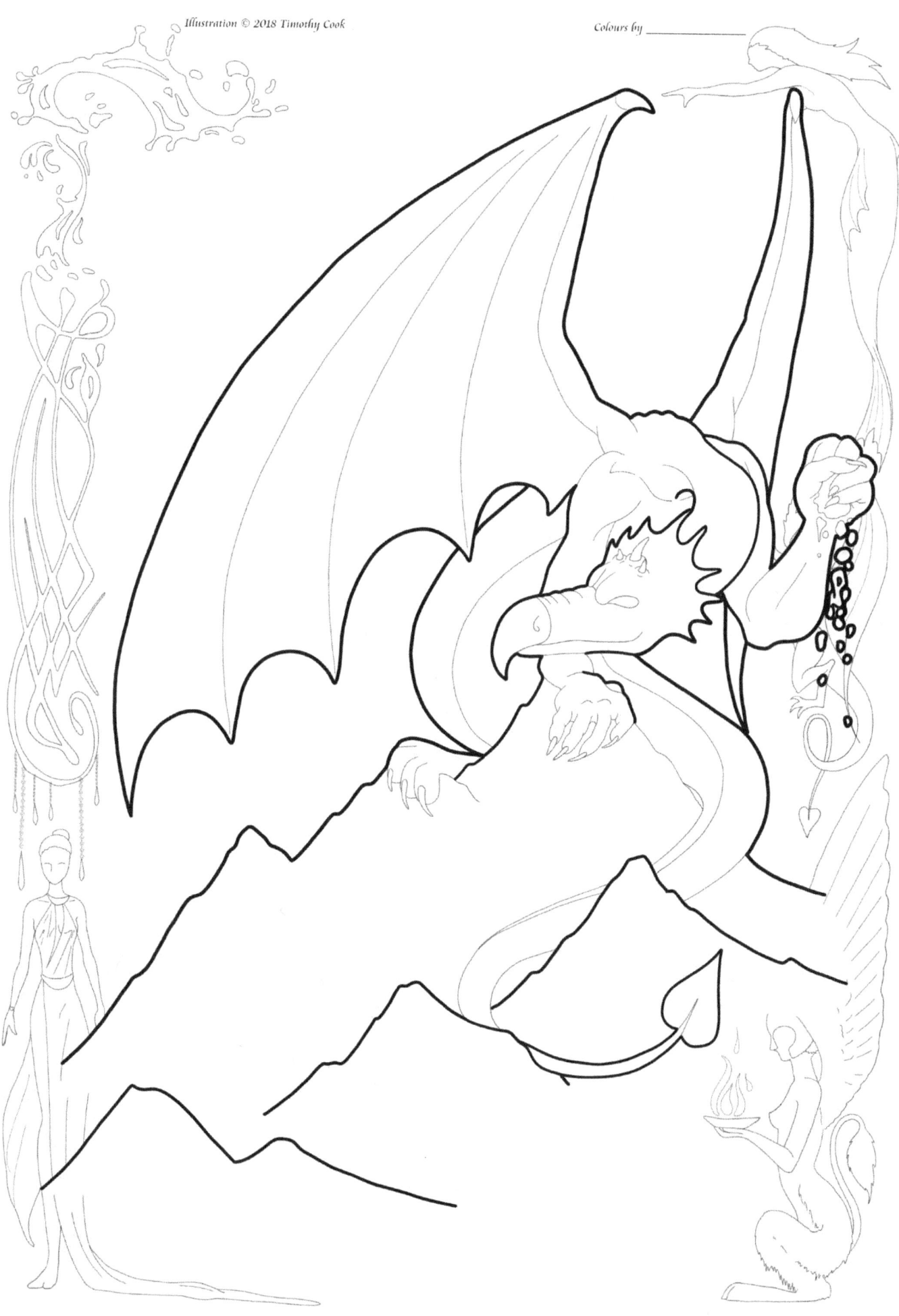

Illustration © 2018 Timothy Cook   Colours by _____

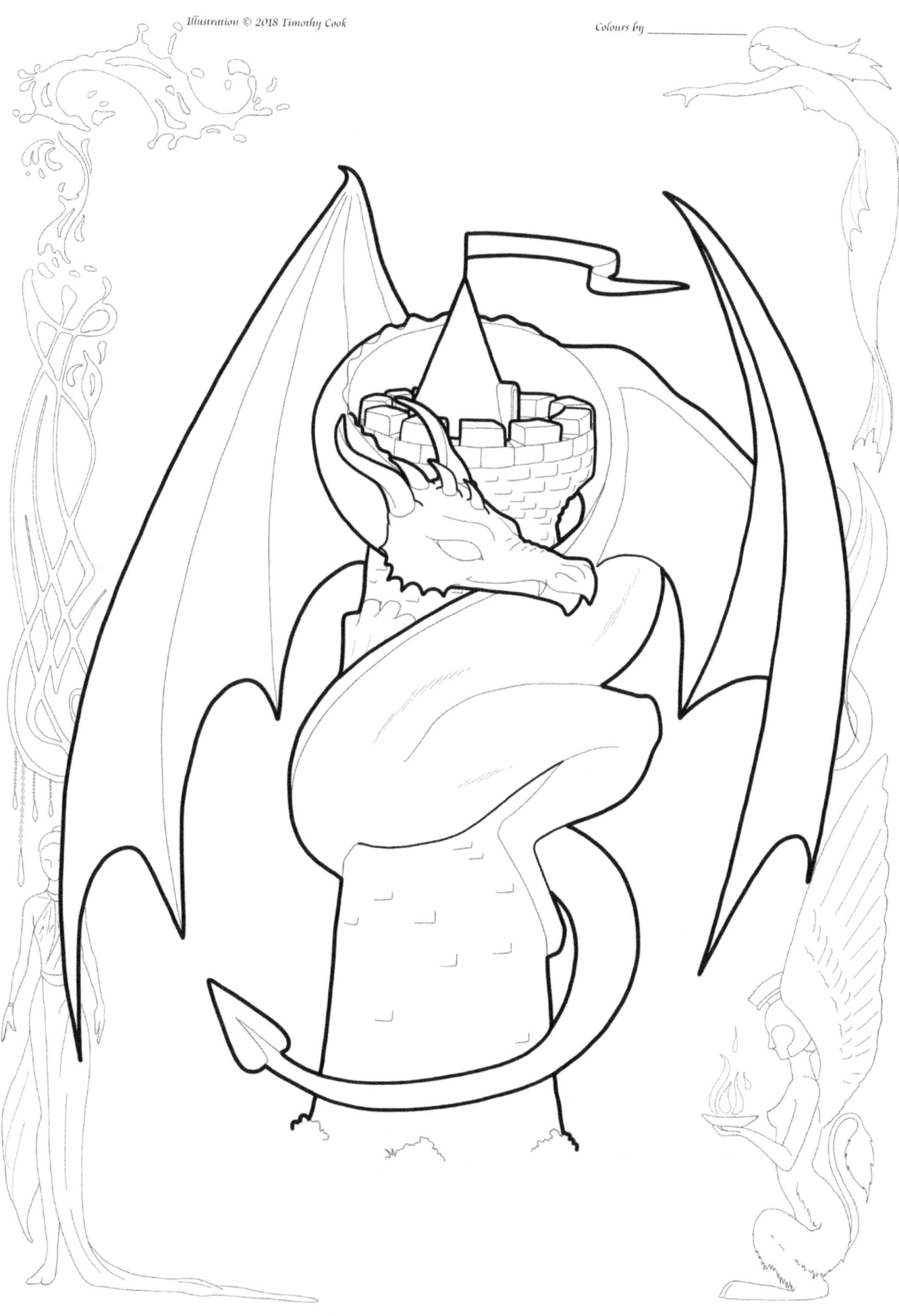

Illustration © 2018 Timothy Cook   Colours by _____

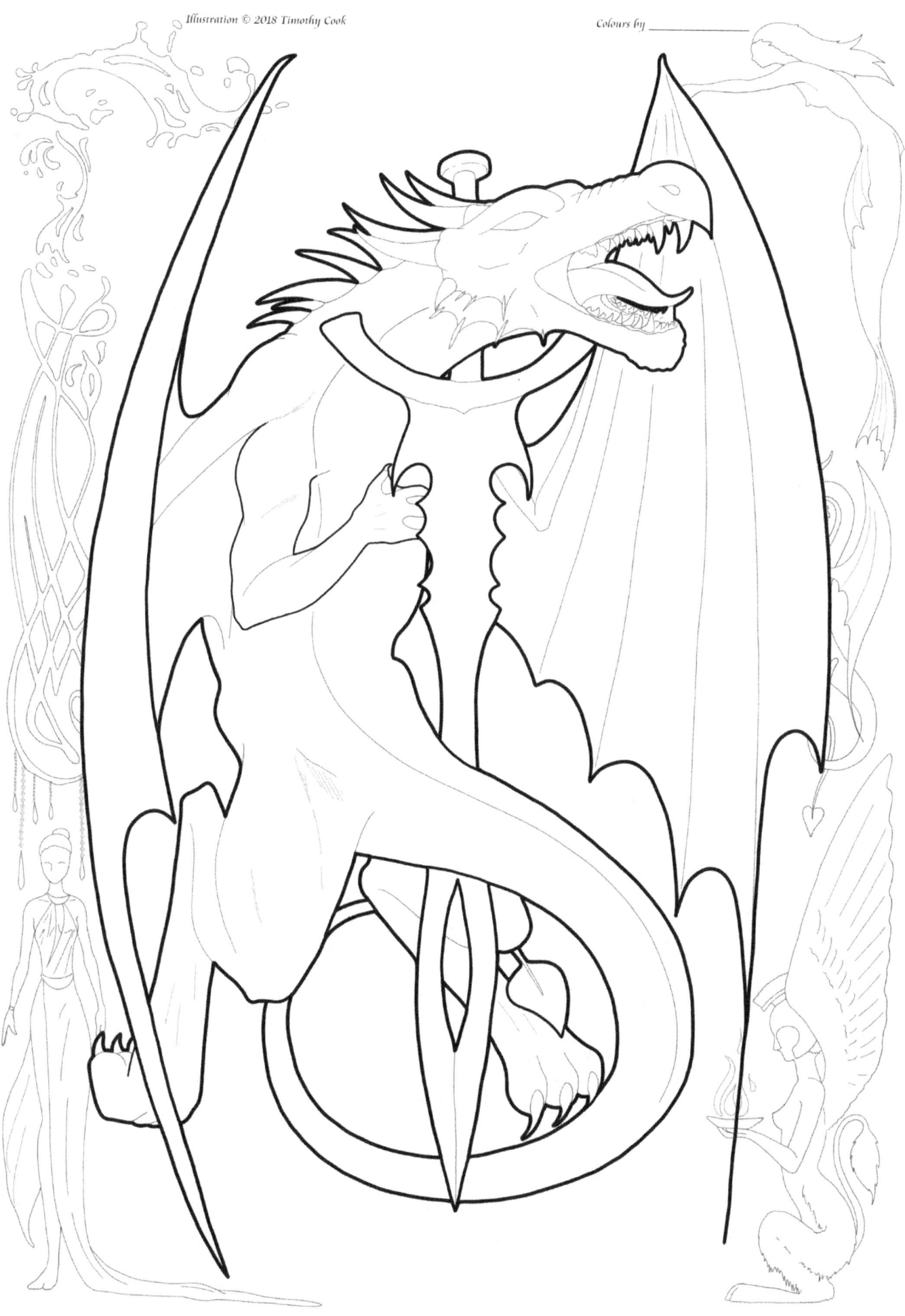

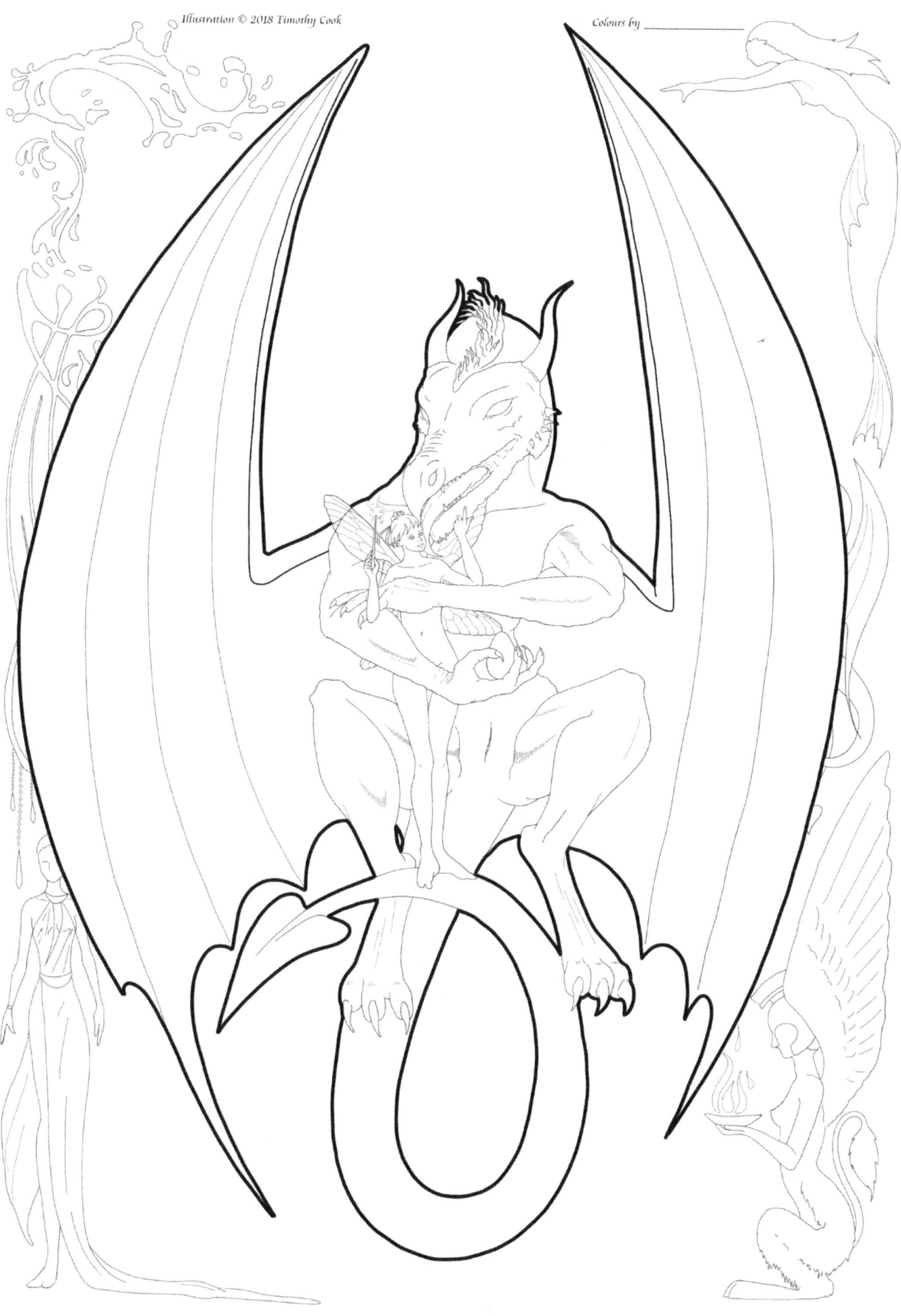

Illustration © 2018 Timothy Cook   Colours by _____

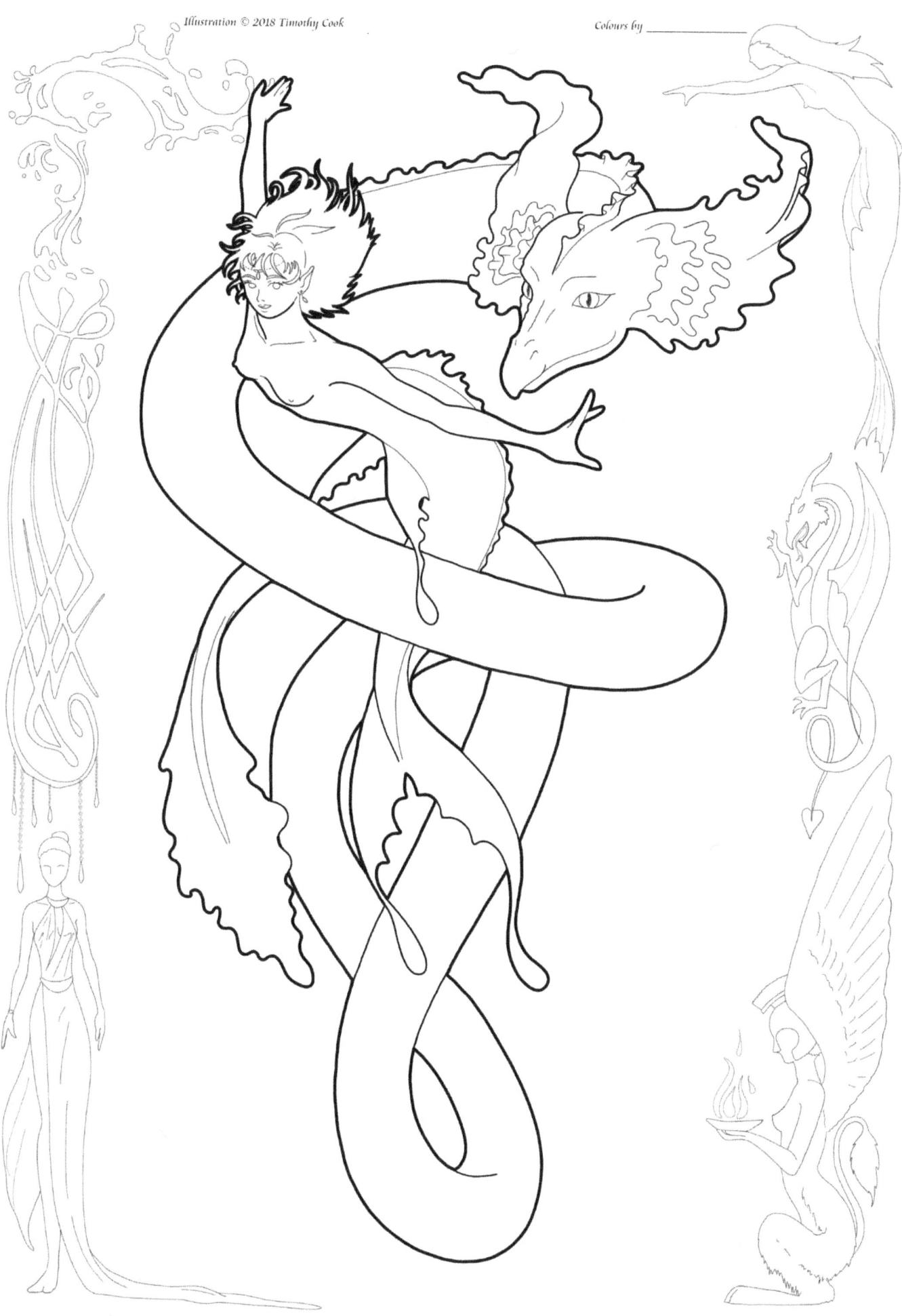

Illustration © 2018 Timothy Cook   Colours by _____

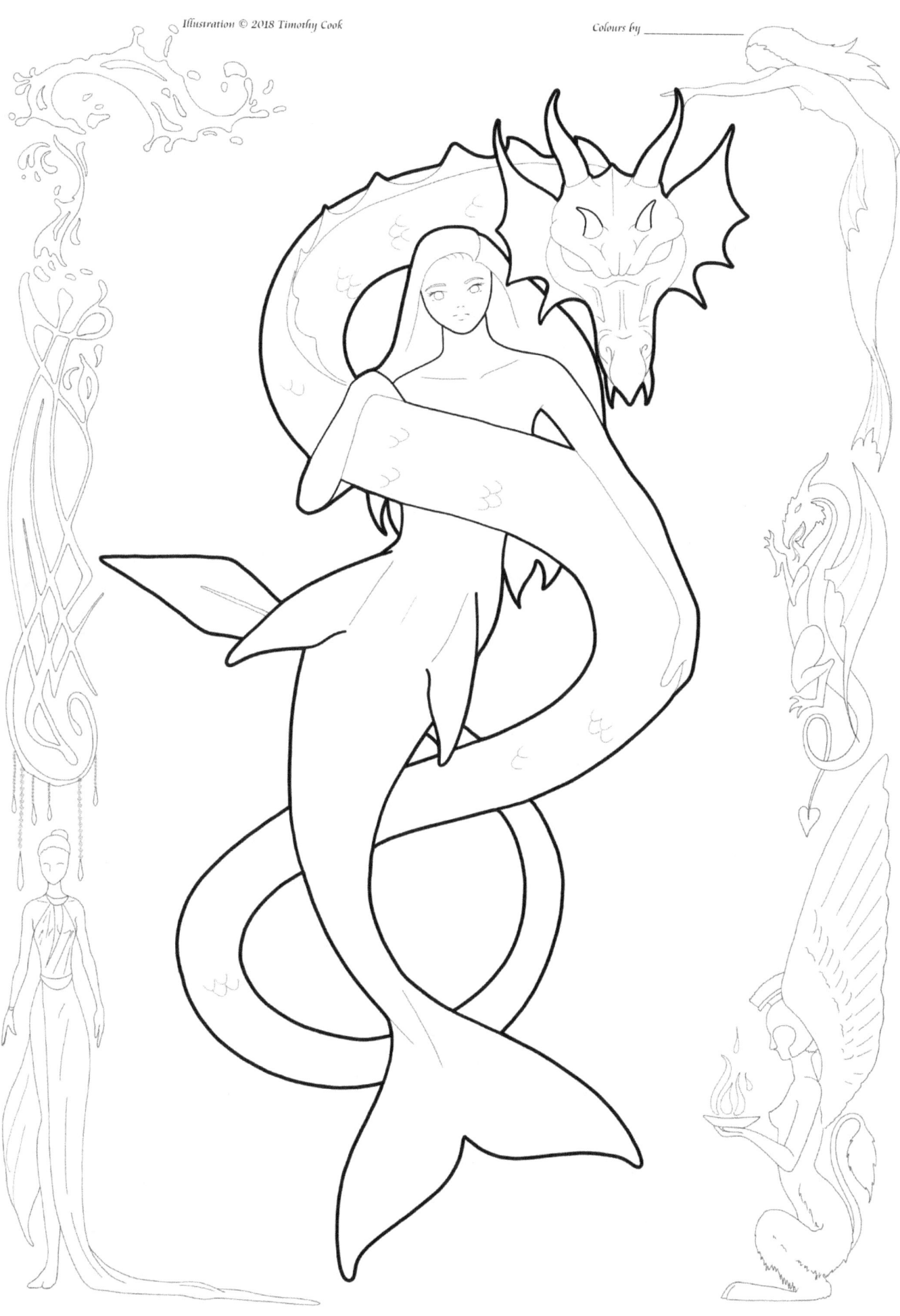

Illustration © 2018 Timothy Cook   Colours by _____

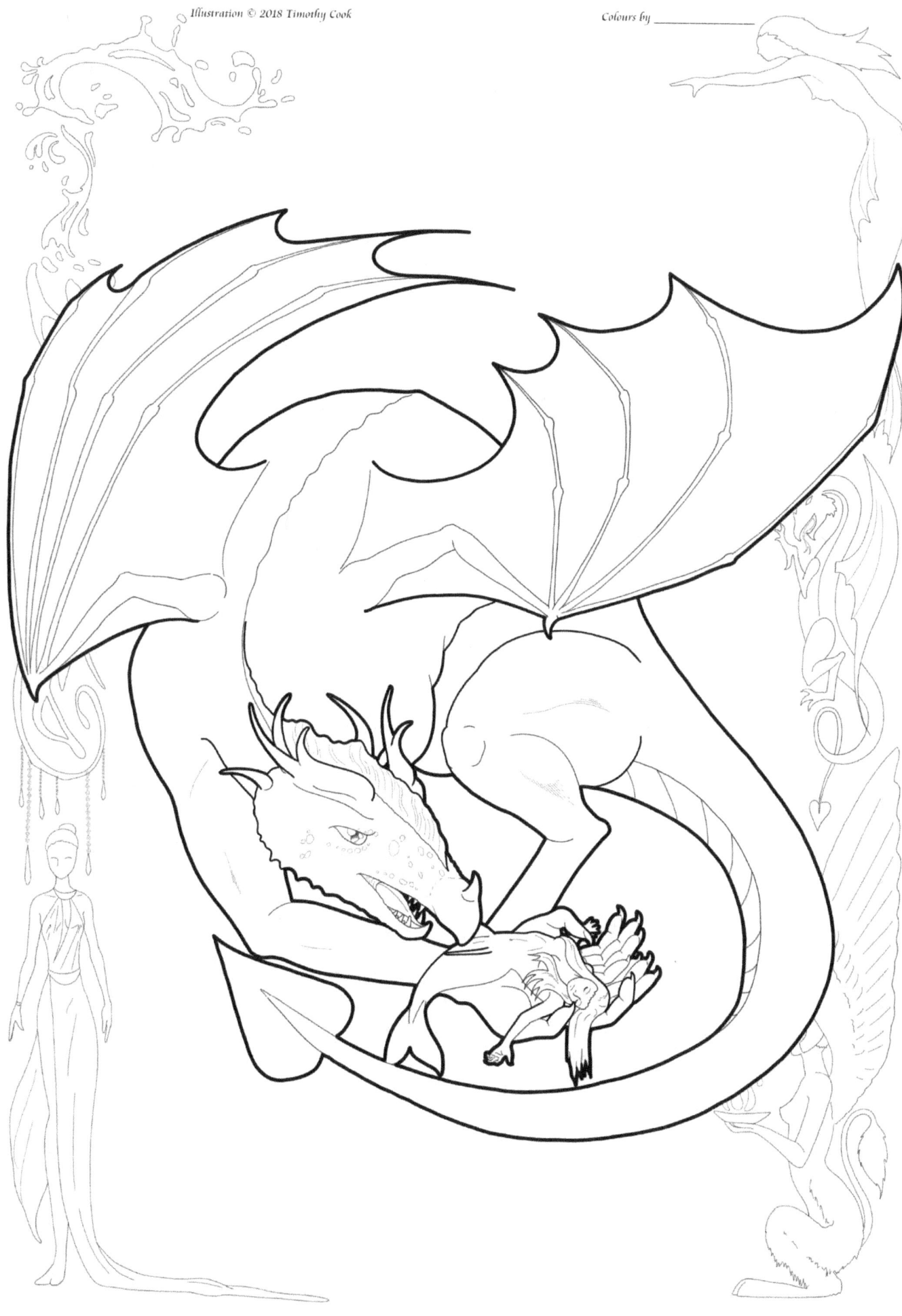

Illustration © 2018 Timothy Cook Colours by _____

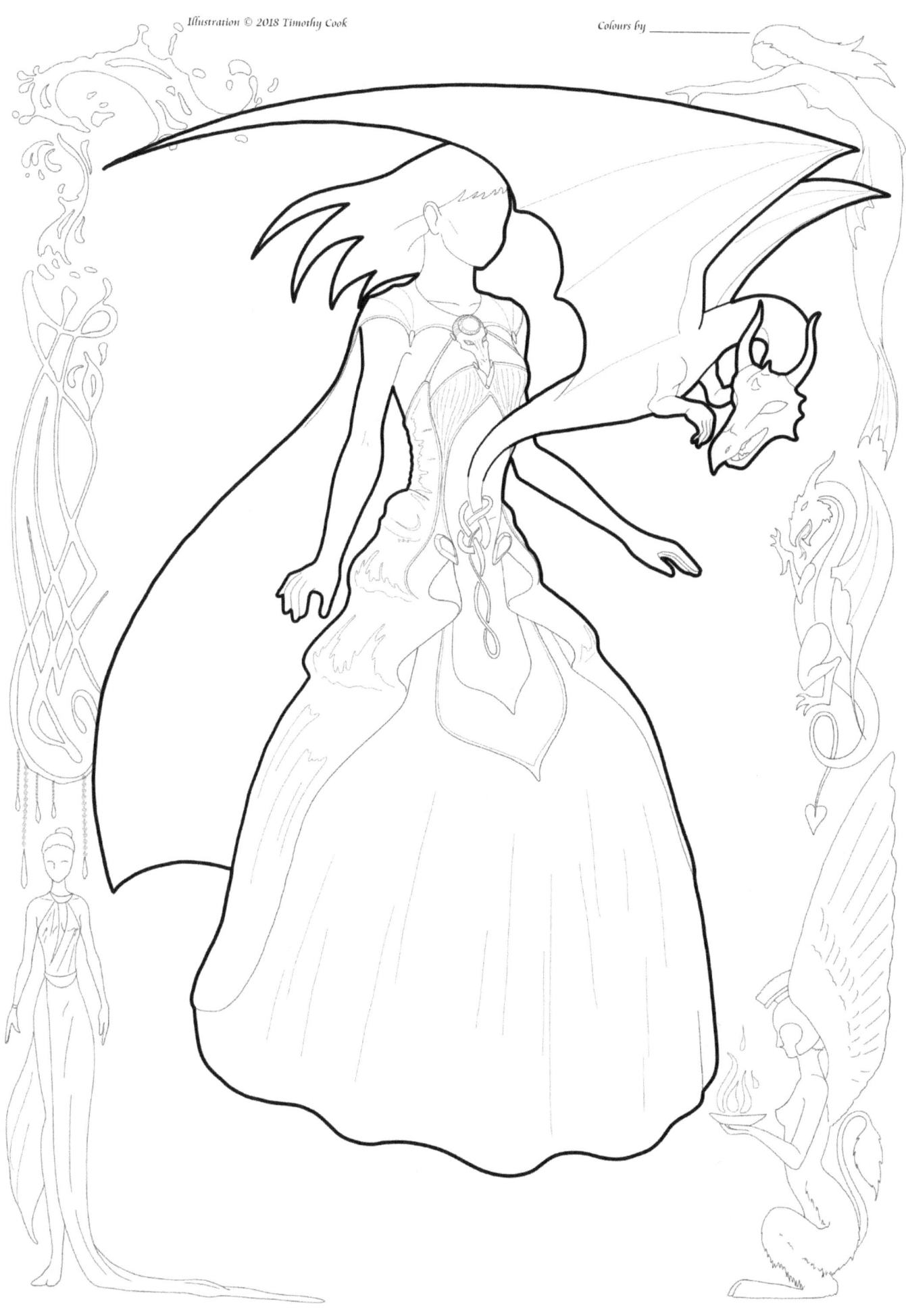

Part IV

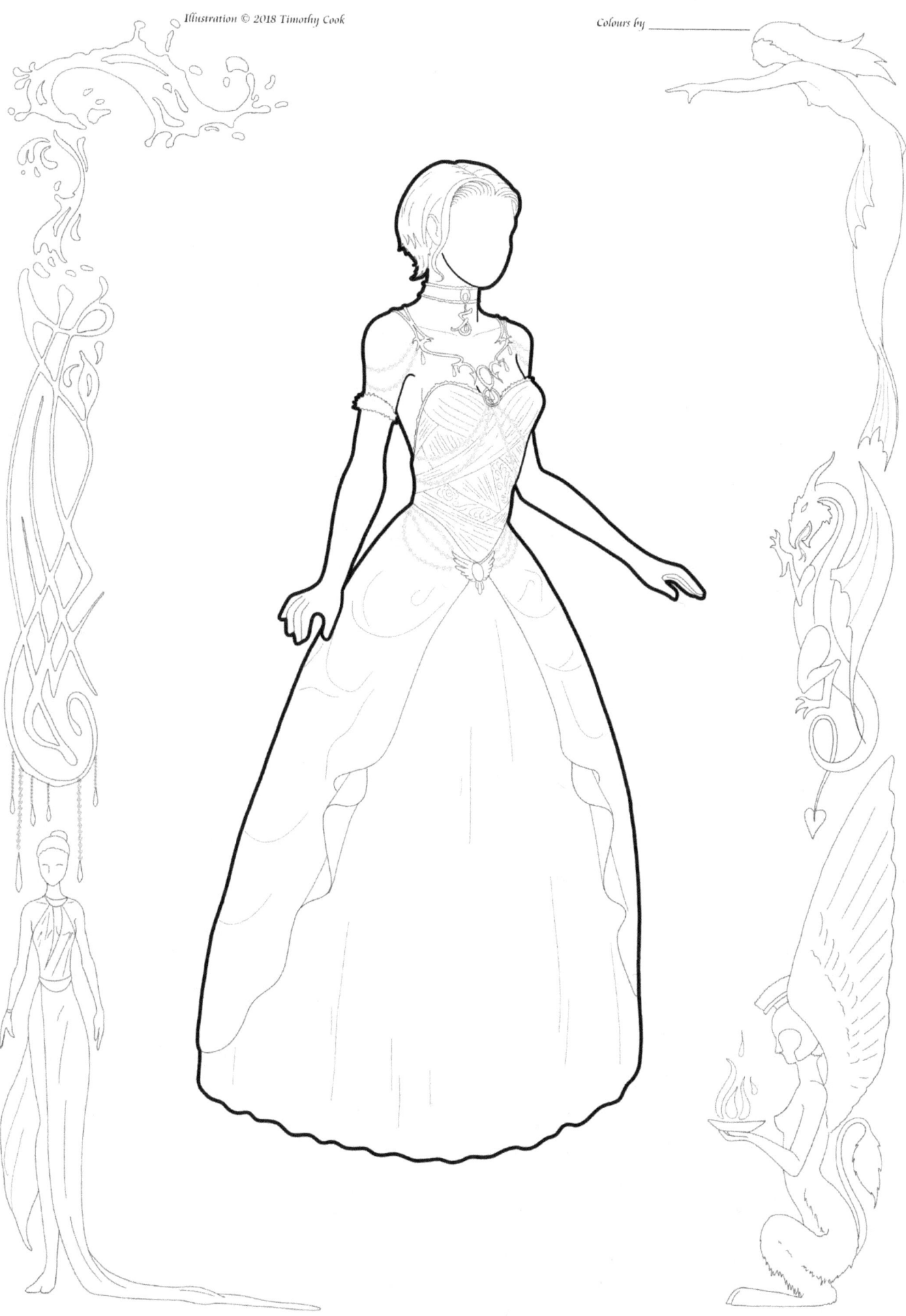

Illustration © 2018 Timothy Cook   Colours by _____

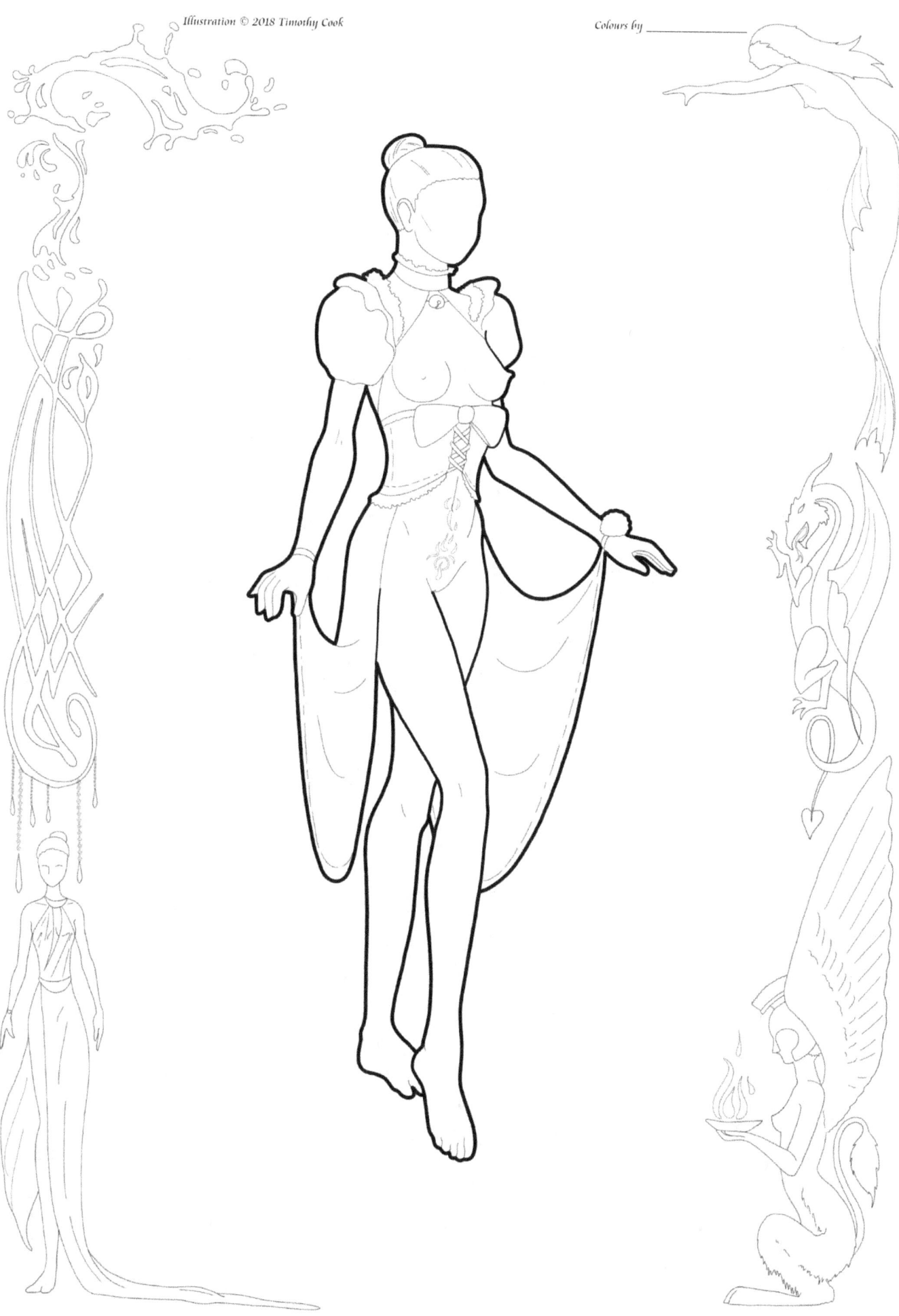

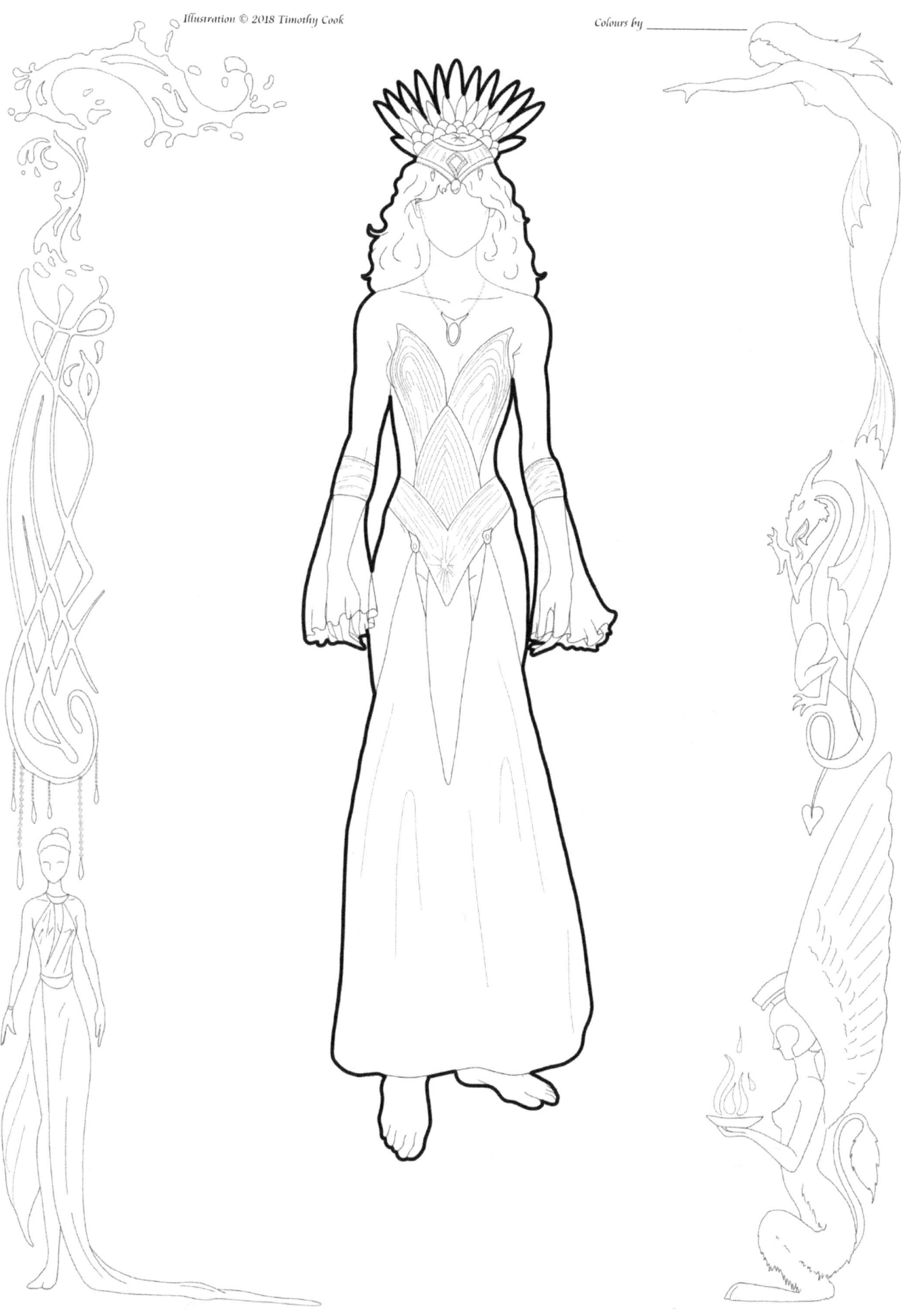

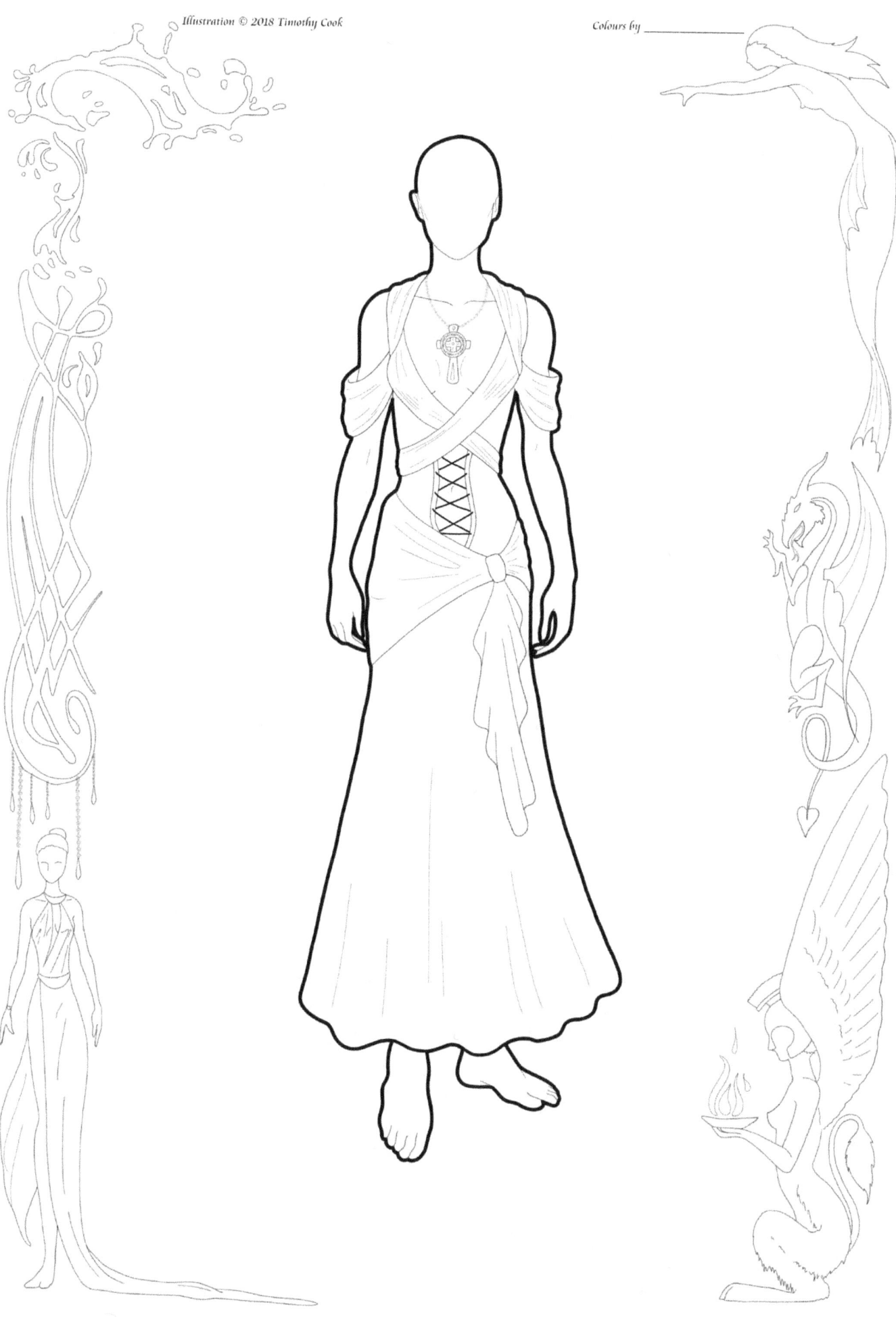

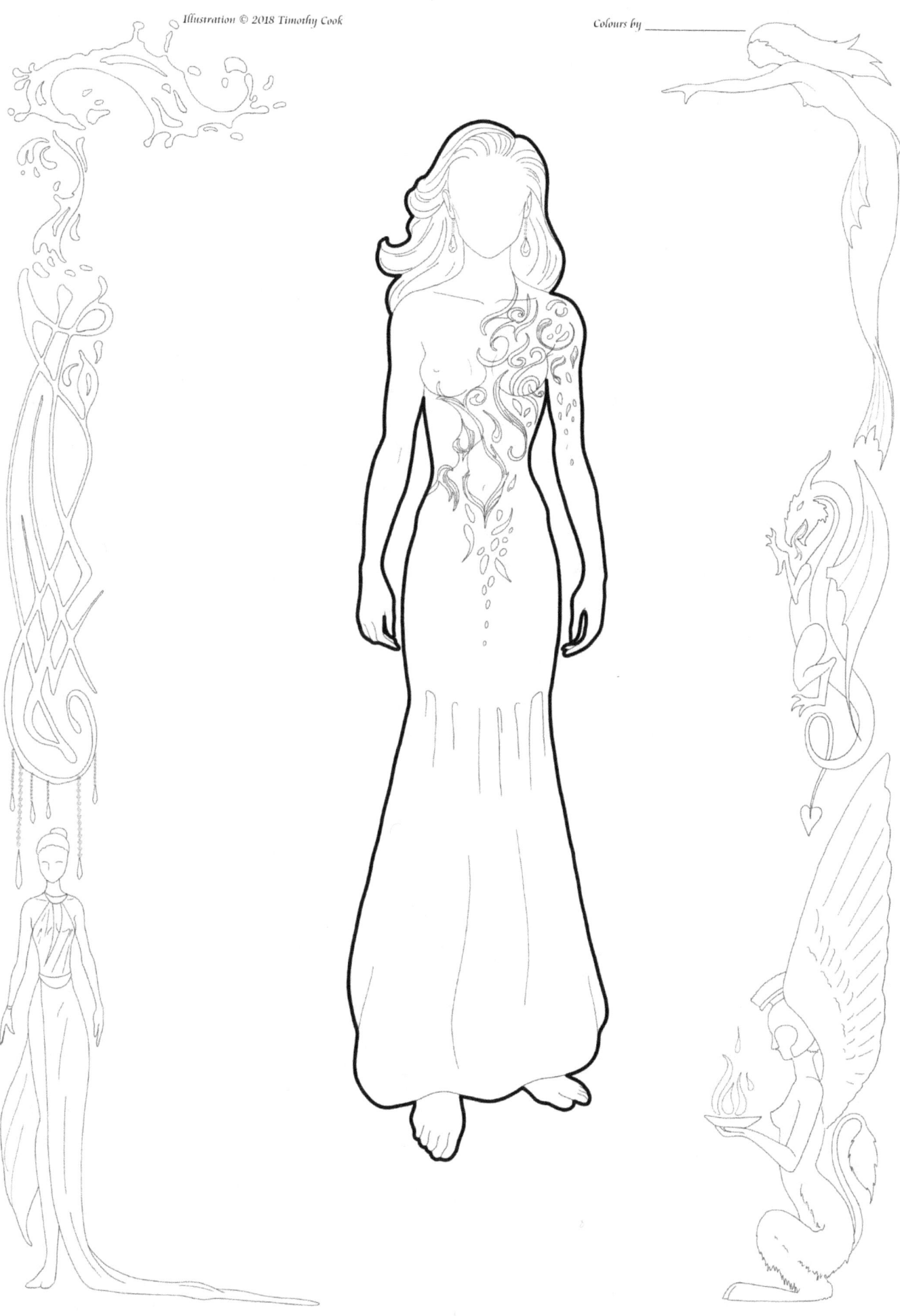

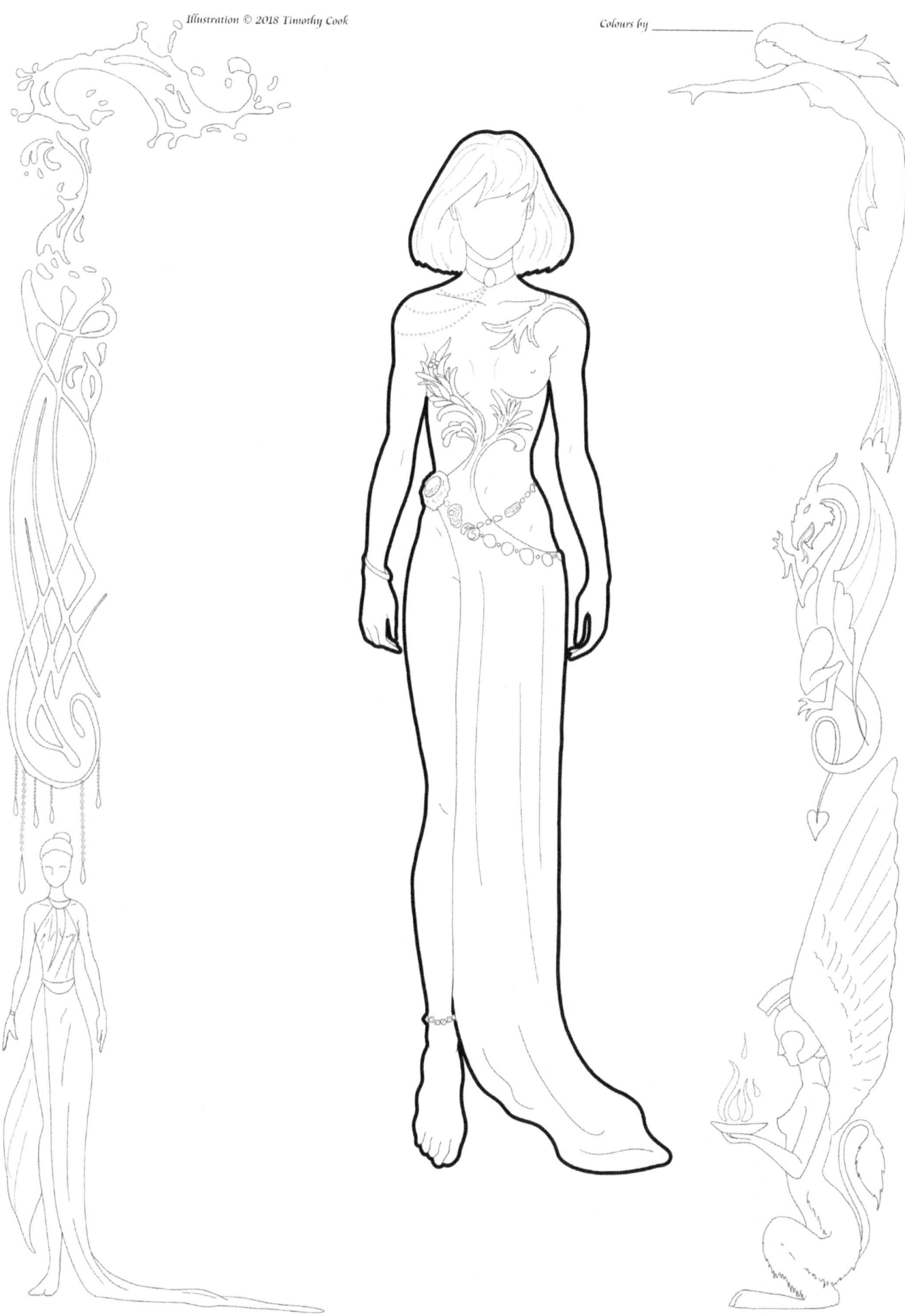

Illustration © 2018 Timothy Cook Colours by _____

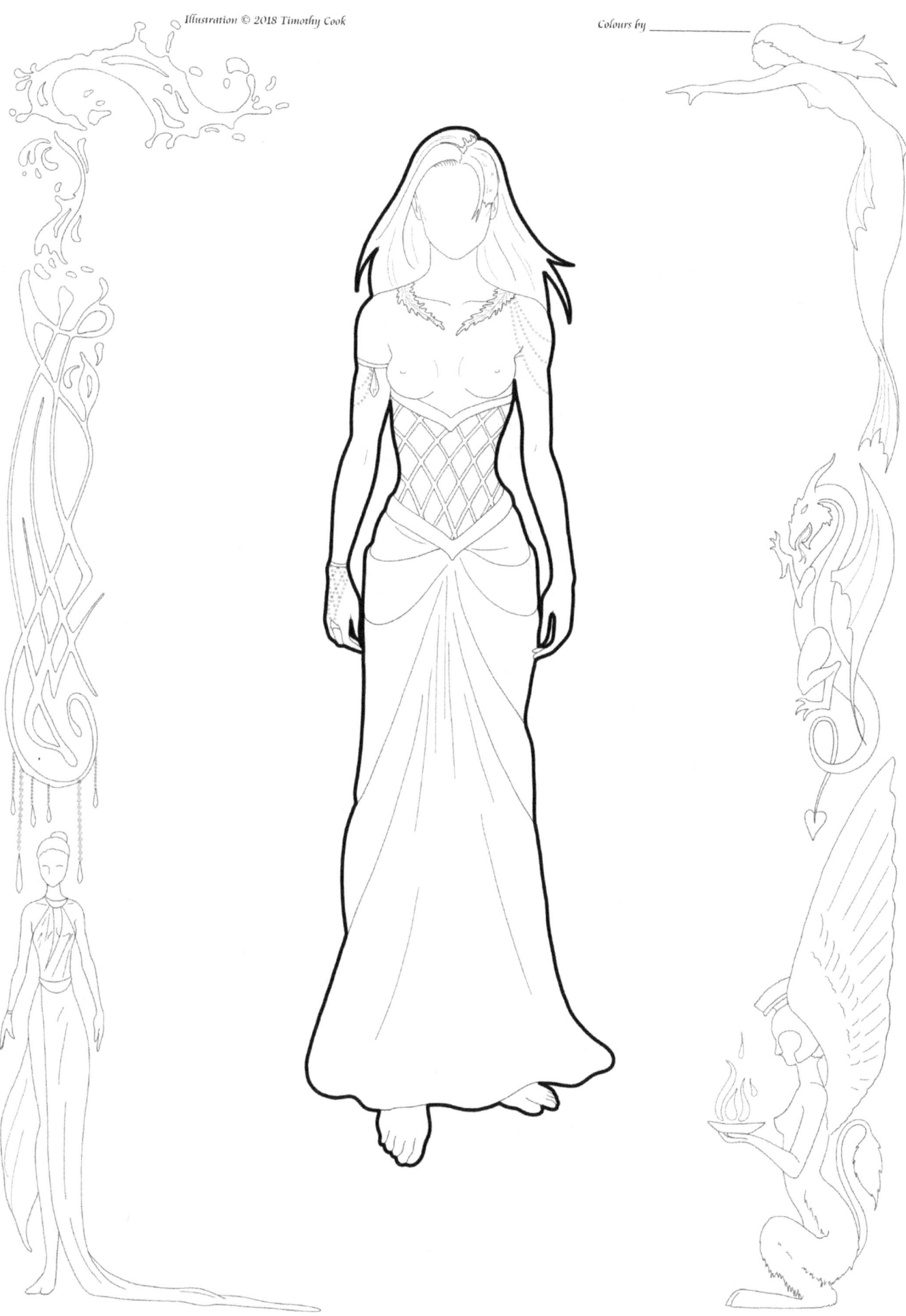

Illustration © 2018 Timothy Cook Colours by _____

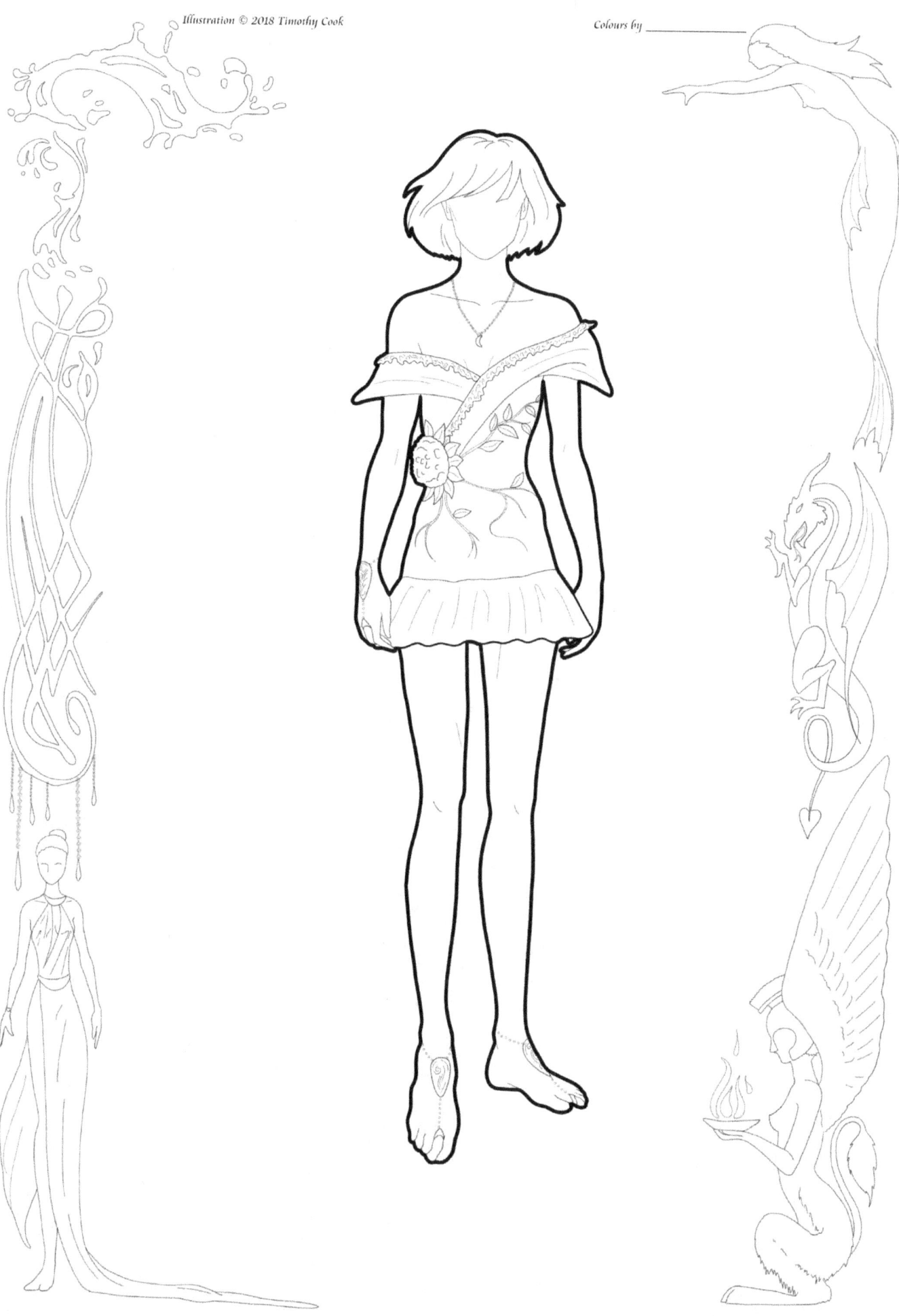

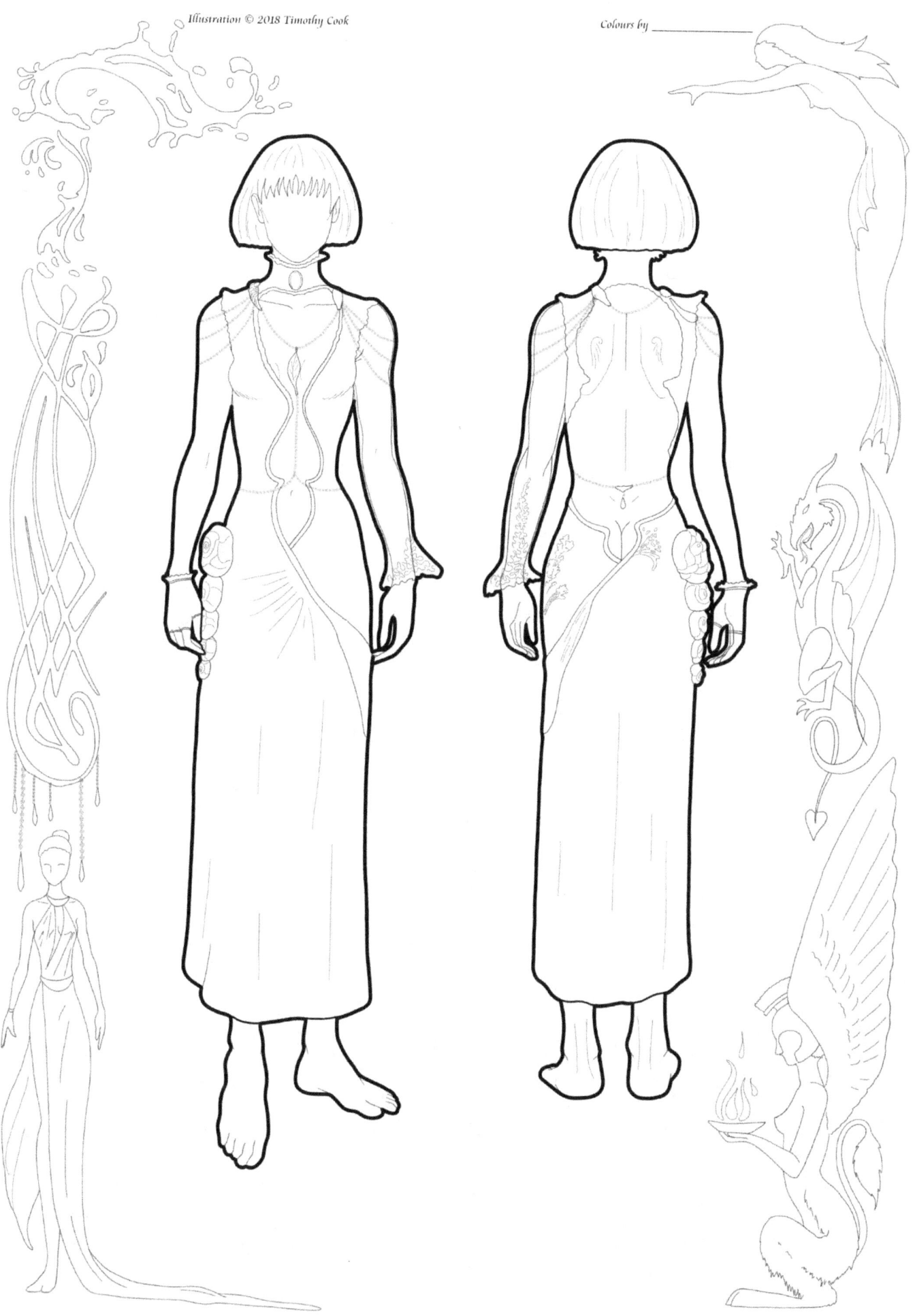

Illustration © 2018 Timothy Cook *Colours by* _____

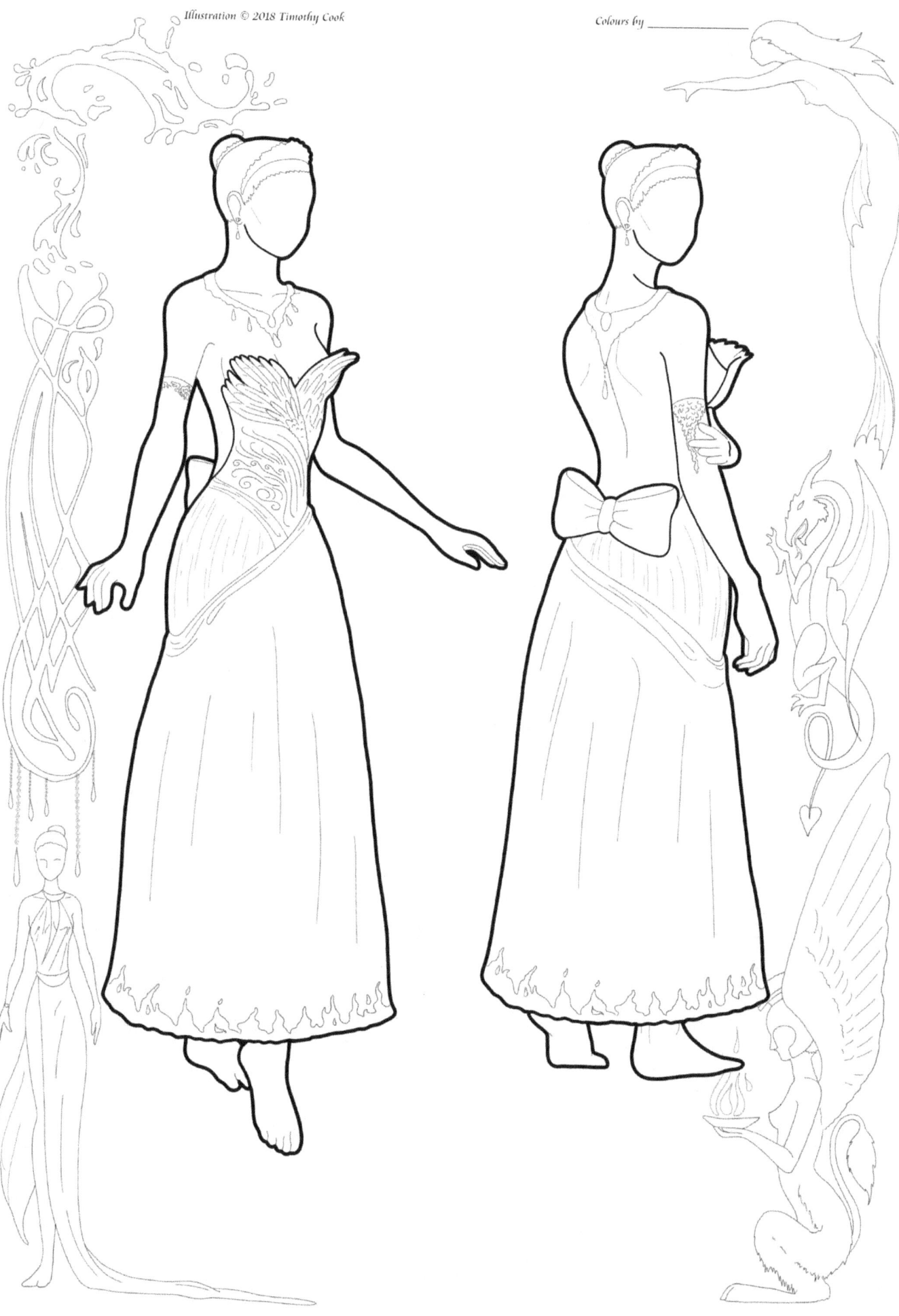

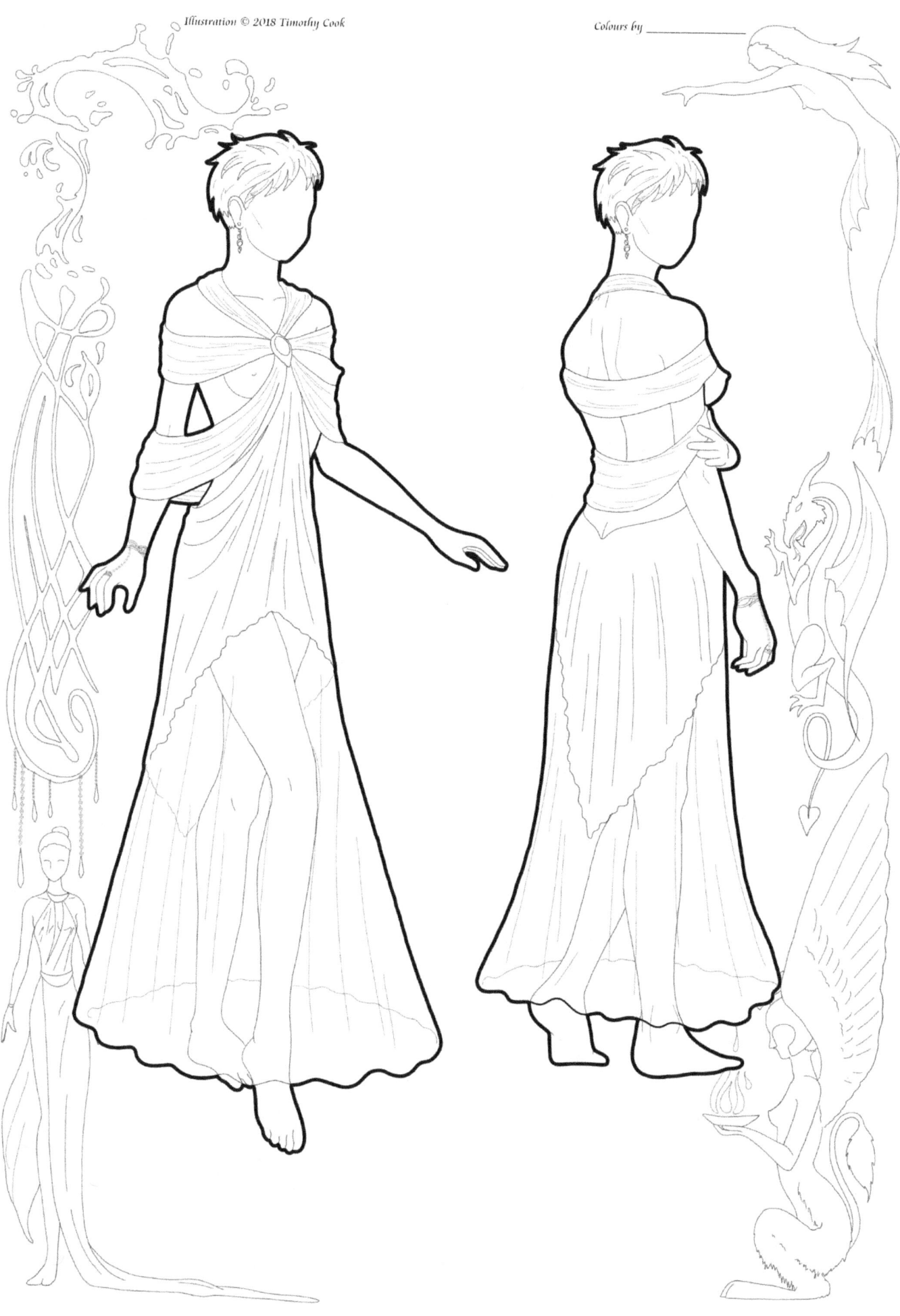

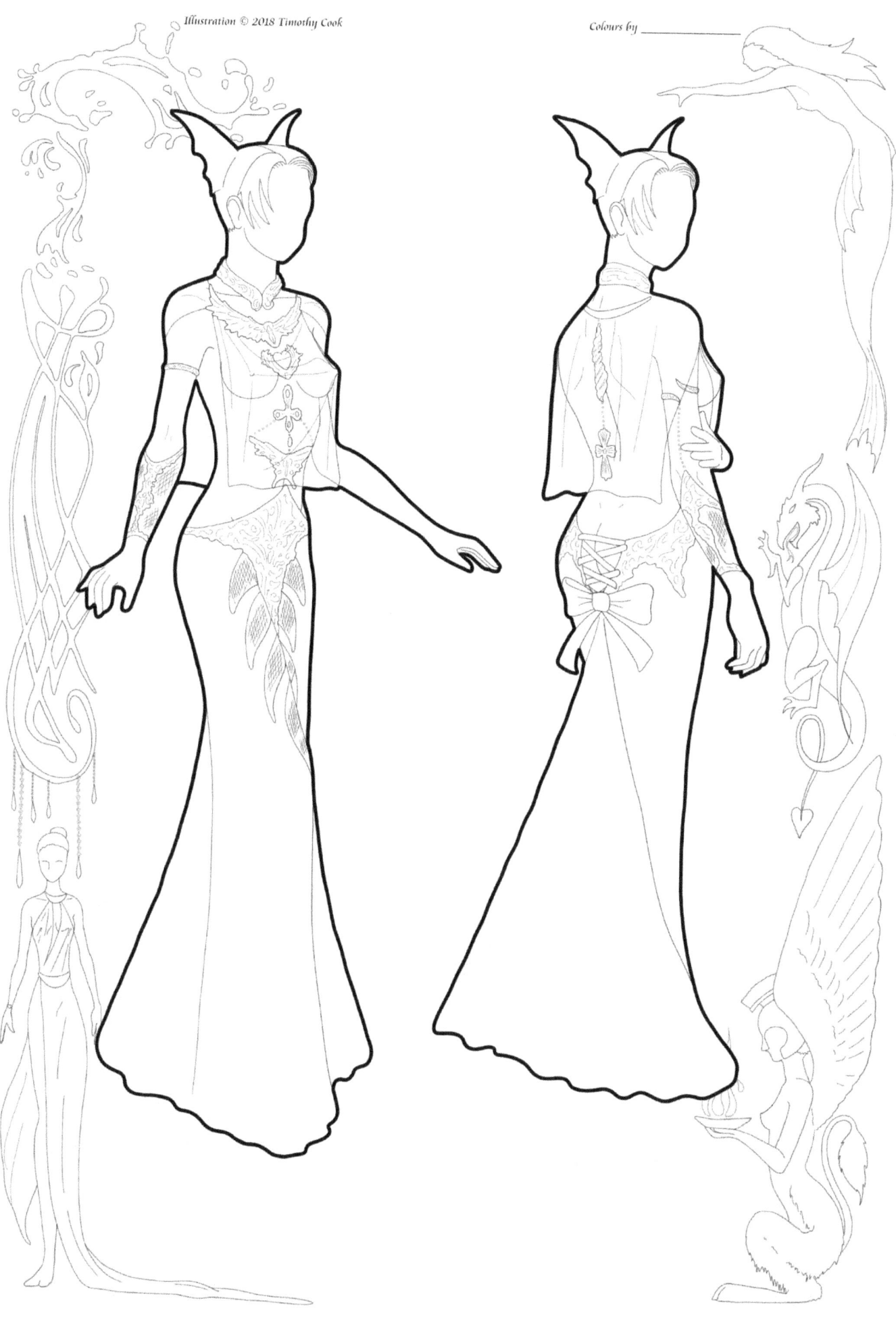

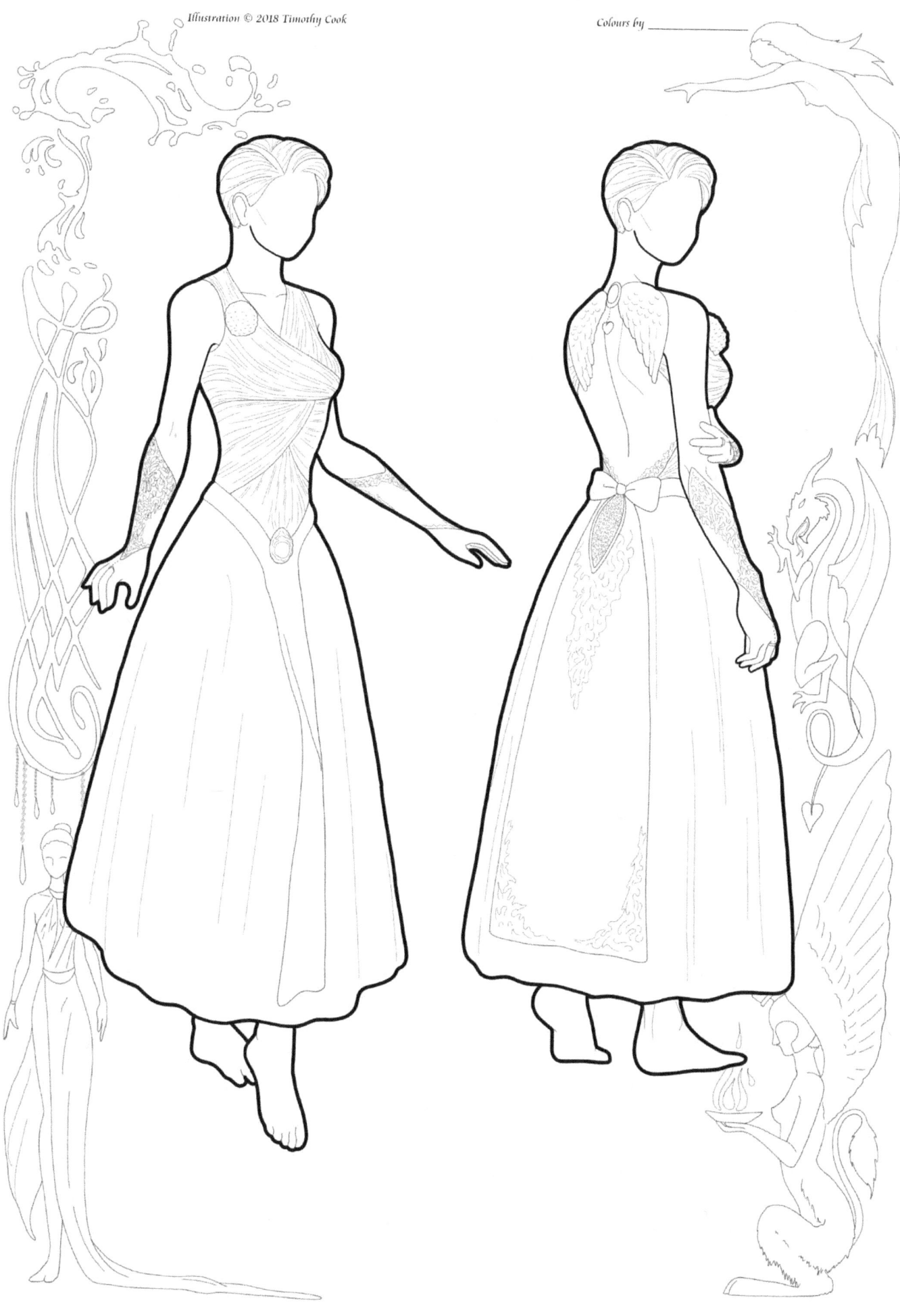

Illustration © 2018 Timothy Cook   Colours by _____

Illustration © 2018 Timothy Cook   Colours by _____

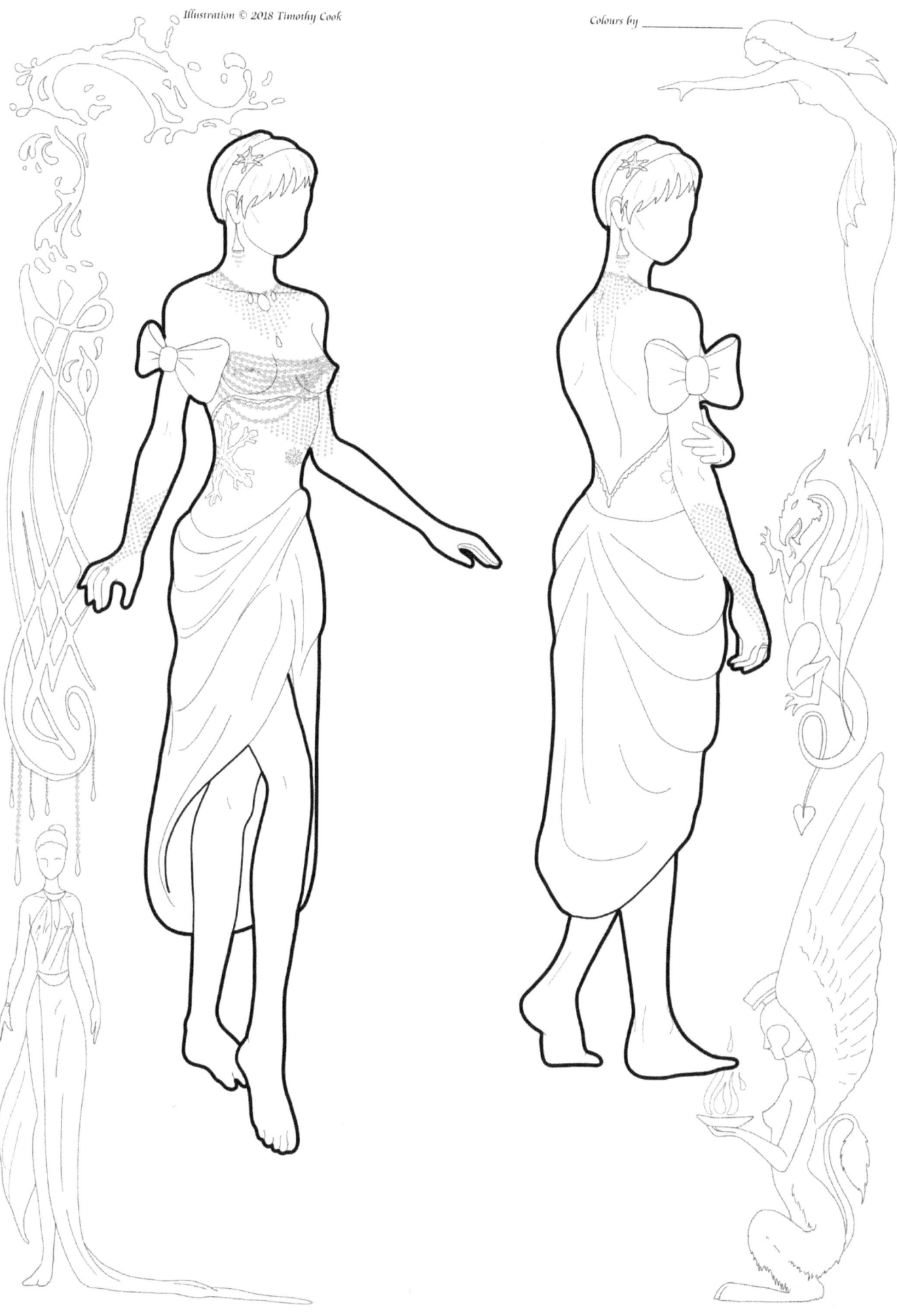

www.ingramcontent.com/pod-product-compliance
Lightning Source LLC
Chambersburg PA
CBHW081018240526
45471CB00017B/3278